Tuesday at Dawn

Stories and Advice from
Rebbetzin
Batsheva Kanievsky ע״ה

As told first-hand to
Ruth Attias

סדור
תפלת כלפה
עם הקריאות
אוסכנו

שמור
לרבנית קנייבסקי

Originally published in Hebrew as *Shlishi b'Ashmores* (2011)

TRANSLATED INTO ENGLISH BY:
Sheindel Weinbach

GRAPHIC LAYOUT BY:
Dimyon

TYPESETTING:
Eden Chachamtzedek

ISBN 978-1-60763-089-0

Copyright © 2012 by R. Attias

13 Rav Dessler St.
Bnei Brak, Israel 51508
tel: 972-3-618-6798
email: bill@dimyon.biz

DISTRIBUTED BY:

The Judaica Press, Inc.
123 Ditmas Avenue | Brooklyn, NY 11218
800-972-6200 | Fax 718-972-6204
info@judaicapress.com
judaicapress.com

Printed in Israel

Contents

A Letter from the Rebbetzin's son-in-law
Hagaon R' Zelig Braverman *shlita*

BS"D *erev* Shabbos *kodesh Parshas Lech Lecha,*
"The souls they made…"

TESTIMONIAL

At the beginning of the year, when we came to receive blessings for the new year, the Rebbetzin *a"h* sat us down, as usual, asking us to hear her stories — wondrous tales of the souls she made [and saved], stories of deliverance, about the power of Shabbos, of guarding one's tongue and more.

One story followed fast upon another as the Rebbetzin talked on at random, spouting stories the likes of which had been heard in this room by the hundreds.

I asked her: "Why must these stories be lost to posterity? Why shouldn't they be recorded for the coming generations?"

And she replied: "Indeed. Mrs. Attias comes to me each Tuesday at dawn and transcribes my stories in writing."

We left the house, silence reigning in the night, reflecting the awe of the coming Judgment. Just then, we met the Attias family and told them what we had just heard from the Rebbetzin. Never did she, nor we, dream that so soon [after that conversation] I would be called upon to corroborate [the Rebbetzin's words].

I read the stories, presented here very authentically, creating the feeling that a one-person audience was standing right before us.

May Hashem grant that this endeavor serve its beneficial purpose, as the Rebbetzin desired all her days.

Written in tears

Z. Braverman

"קולם" דברי אמת"

בריא היו שתעו, נפשתינן לחתברנך לשנה טובה, רקיתי
וירקיית עד כרכב תשיר להסר ולאושן סיגורים. סיגורי
לשלוש יד הנפש אשר שלנה, סיגורי ישולע, יד כחה ש
שבר, ש שאס וכה וכו'.

סיגורי חדל סיגור, והרגיש את לוצושה, סיגורים ישלו שלוש
לאשוא שקיני יה.

שלטיניה: ואנוך שולט לובבון, אבוק אול יראו וירעוצו לשבון שולים?
אם היו שעני, ולק, הגל שולטלוס לצה ש שיש לוכחוות ורושאת
אי שיגורים אל שון.

כרתינן שנגרת ולאמאת שנרית שד, שאושאת שתורת הבן, שלין השלק שולשים
שיעול לצם את אשר שקע שד שרני שני הרקית.

אם שלנה היו, ולון שיגל ולוני, אשרקעון לאמאן עד שבאי: כב שוני.
לשבון ג. לקיוו את הסילורים, שסורים הויקשיויר ולוקיע את הקמושו
שולין כלשה שאושן. שואת ולשרת לשע שיניל.
יין ג' ויה לקועלת שקיני. שלשין ש הושם

וכתבת שלינו
ג' כאושן

A Letter from the Rebbetzin's son
Hagaon R' Yitzchak Shaul Kanievsky *shlita*

BH"Y *erev* Shabbos *kodesh*
Vayishlach, Kislev 5772

To the Esteemed *Hagaon* R' Avraham Attias *shlita*

I write my feelings as a son, regarding the new book, *Shlishi b'Ashmores* (*Tuesday at Dawn*), having skimmed through it and read several of its passages.

Whoever reads the stories of my righteous mother *a"h*, conveyed in her very pure and holy words, can derive worlds of benefit — each according to his spiritual level. The more elevated the reader, the deeper s/he can internalize their messages, absorb their purity and holiness and be strengthened in *emunah* and *bitachon*, love for Torah and *histapkus b'muat* (sufficiency with the minimum), as well as all the other worthy *middos*. That, after all, is how people were affected in her proximity during her lifetime, day by day.

By incorporating all these aspects in this book, you have lifted up the pure soul of my righteous mother to a very high place, indeed, and she will surely intercede for you and for all of her offspring and dear ones before the Heavenly Throne. Thus may we merit seeing the ultimate *geulah* together with all of *Klal Yisrael*, Amen!

Written with deep appreciation
Yitzchak Shaul Kanievsky

שלום רב אלי מרים פסח גוליק

לכבוד הגליל הנפלא מירושלים בלבבי

אבקשך לבדק הדבר הזה ואף זה רחוק מן הדבר הספר ראשונה נכתבה והראשונה אחרי
שאינה כפי פרטים מספר

נפלינו של הספרים עד אני של לצרכי רב ולהלן הרבה והדבר פה אחרון
אות הרבה עולות ישנה יחד בה יותר נפש זו רבות פסים ויד
בליה והרה ורה פה אולם בואון ולהראות תורה והסתלקות רבה
ופה נעשים נפל זה הוא אמנו בימי עולם.

ופעלתינו פי על רסף ורף הלא עולם את נפשם והרבה ורהבהורה זו ואינו אות אף
הכבה הגליל נפשות רבות אתן והגו סוגים ולשביליה רבות
לפי כבה הכבה עולות ולררום ביבר של שוליביה ואנוריה ולהו
נפלו זה נפלה הבה אינו זה על של רבה שליל
הכלא אמנן והרב הזר ארוכה פנסך כולו

לברוכך
לשרק

Preface

BEFORE DAWN, AT FIVE A.M., most Bnei Brak residents are still sleeping, or are just beginning to open their eyes to greet the new day — but not everyone...

In the home of Rebbetzin Batsheva Kanievsky on Rechov Rashbam, the day has long since begun. Darkness has been banished even before the crack of dawn.

Very quietly, unobtrusively, women have already slipped into the *ezras nashim* of the famous Lederman shul, the favored shul of Torah giants past and present, among them Maran the Steipler *zy"a* and his son, *ylcht"a, Hagaon* R' Chaim Kanievsky *shlita*.

There, in the old and familiar room, its walls steeped with infinite prayers, blessings, wishes, hopes from hearts overflowing with love and showered with countless dew-drops of devotion for Hashem, His Torah and His people — these women come to add their own prayers to all of those who came before them. Utter silence reigns in the large room, even though it begins filling up to the bursting point. But its walls retain their reverent stillness, imposing it upon the people within. In the women's gallery is a side table, around which most of the women are huddled.

That is where the Rebbetzin sat.

Her lips moved ceaselessly, conveying intense concentration. Her daily scheme of prayers: *Iggeres HaRambam; Tehillim, Nishmas, Perek Shirah* and the *birchos hashachar.* The latter recital was an entire uplifting experience of its own. The Rebbetzin recited the blessing to the avid audience of women who replied "*Amen*" with full passion. Then each woman stood, in turn, recited the *berachos* out loud, waiting for the effusive "*Amen*" of the rest. "Only when someone answers '*Amen*' to your *berachah* is it complete," the Rebbetzin repeatedly explained.

Kvitlach were pressed into her hand in an ongoing flow, some intended for her blessing while others were meant to be passed on to her husband, *Hagaon* R' Chaim. And when she did so, later, she invariably appended her own hearty blessing.

Her tender heart was wounded and bruised from all the *tzaros* people suffer and poured out before her receptive ears, day after day. Yet she gave everyone her full attention, listening with the empathy of a first-time audience. She listened with her heart and soul, oblivious to the speaker's outward appearance or where she was coming from.

Again and again, she was the ear to long tales of suffering, pain and hardship from women who came from all over, pouring out their hearts and begging for a blessing that would put an end to their misery.

The Rebbetzin showered them with her comforting benedictions that fell like refreshing dew, sincere blessings from the heart, issuing from a deep love for her people. They encouraged and heartened, like reviving water on parched earth.

Her attentiveness was legendary. She never tired of listening and sharing people's burdens, and when her turn came to react, she showered each visitor with fresh and effusive encouragement blended with *emunah* and *bitachon* that things would improve.

The Rebbetzin told me that she once turned to her illustrious father, Maran *Hagaon* R' Yosef Shalom Elyashiv *shlita,* and said, "Abba, so many people seek my blessings and I provide these always from the bottom of my heart. But please bless me, Abba, that my *berachos* be effective!"

And her great father did, indeed, grant her plea.

Since then, whenever she visited her father at Yom Tov time, he again buttressed his original blessing that her prayers and wishes for others be fulfilled.

She blessed and blessed, and continued to bless — through innumerous utterings. And her words did, indeed, carry clout in Heaven, for the women continued to come, confident of being helped. And when they came back, many were smiling from ear to ear, conveying their thanks and praise to Hashem for supernatural succor as a result of her blessings and prayers. They thanked her, as well, for her guidance in tailoring the right *kabbalos,* the resolutions which they accepted upon themselves in order to be worthy receptacles for those miracles.

Some visitors were excited *kallos* who came in their snowy white wedding dresses to be blessed on the day of their nuptials. Everyone made way for these special visitors and waived their turn. The Rebbetzin would be no less excited and emotional, as she heaped blessings upon the heads of these brides, while intertwining messages of *chizuk* and wise counsel about the role of a Jewish wife, the wife of a

Torah scholar, and a future "mother in Israel."

Another frequent scene was that of a bas-mitzvah girl receiving a gift from the Rebbetzin, a *sefer* on strengthening her *middos* and *yiras Shamayim*. Yet the Rebbetzin did not suffice with just the gift; she had the recipient wait while she painstakingly wrote a personal dedication, addressed to the girl by name.

❖   ❖   ❖

We go back to resume our *vasikin Shacharis* session with the Rebbetzin, as she follows along with her husband's *minyan*, the morning dew still glistening all about, and the world just beginning to rub its eyes awake. Such a *Shacharis* is an unforgettable and powerful experience.

The *davening* over, the Rebbetzin is escorted by some of the women through a shortcut to her home. A shortcut which ends up being a long way, thanks to the pearls of wisdom which she spouts so effortlessly and naturally, her escorts listening attentively to each and every word. She tells amazing stories of *chizuk* and attests to the veracity of every detail. Each word is a perfect treasure.

I have been privileged to collate some of these treasures, writing them as I heard them directly from her mouth, following the *tefillas vasikin* of "Tuesday at Dawn." My hope is that the reader will be enriched by them, as I was. (Editor's note: Isolated passages in some of the stories in this English edition necessitated minor adaptations in the language in order for the stories to flow more smoothly.)

I was fortunate to have the completed manuscript presented to the Rebbetzin yet in her lifetime. It was read aloud to her, to her great satisfaction and approval.

When I informed her that the material was already type-set and ready for printing, she expressed a desire to write a dedication for it. But Hashem had other plans and gathered her soul up to Heaven on Shabbos Chol HaMo'ed Sukkos, the 17th of Tishrei, 5772.

We did not merit to get such a letter, but we presented the Hebrew manuscript to her son, *Hagaon* R' Yitzchak Shaul, who gave it to his father, *Hagaon* R' Chaim. R' Yitzchak Shaul said that his father read the book, enjoyed it and said: "The stories here are true and they can instill much *yiras Shamayim.*"

I pray that this book be to her spiritual advantage above.

Wishing the readers a beneficial
and rewarding reading,
Ruth Attias

Foreword

I SAVORED THE VERY air. There was something pristine and pure about the violet sky above Rechov Rashbam at the break of dawn. I loved hearing the birds twittering as I discerned a white *tallis* materializing from a building through the grey morning mist and heading towards the shul.

In her later years, I made every possible effort to meet her at dawn at least once week — on Tuesday mornings, the day graced with a double "*ki tov.*"

This meeting did me good. It evoked sweet childhood memories of when I grew up in the same neighborhood as the Rebbetzin and her young daughters.

Then, one day, Rebbetzin Kanievsky stroked my hand and said to me, "Ruthy, listen to this amazing story…"

Ever since then, every Tuesday, I stood next to her, writing pad in hand, pen poised to transcribe her words. She spoke and I wrote. Women who came to *daven* and receive her prayers used to gather around us to drink in her words.

"Someday I am going to publish a book," I told her. She loved my writing pad. She would speak and I would write, as she drummed her finger on the pad. At the time, I did not sufficiently appreciate the great gift she was giving me.

When I came to her this past summer with the manuscript almost completed, she took it and reviewed all the stories so familiar to her. Smiling her famous smile, she said, "Wait a bit more…" as if she had a premonition.

This past *erev* Rosh Hashanah, I joined my parents on Rechov Rashbam 19 for the Yom Tov meal. When I left the building, I came upon my friend, Bracha Braverman, the Rebbetzin's daughter, who had dined with her parents. She waved to me and said, "My mother was just talking about you."

About me? At the Rosh Hashanah meal? Strange.

She continued, "You know that my mother is always telling stories, and they have a tremendous impact on the listeners. My husband said to her, 'Ima, you must put out a book with the marvelous stories that happen to you.' And she said, 'Don't worry. Someone is doing just that. Ruthy.'"

Then my friend asked me, "Ruthy, after my mother's 120 years, will you do something with them?"

The book was already close to completion but all I said was, "We'll see."

Who would have thought that our metaphoric "120 years" would come round in a matter of weeks? At that time, I wasn't aware of how precious those pages were, but Divine Providence surely arranged that there be a perpetual memory of her.

With hot tears and searing longings, we bring to publication what the Rebbetzin presented to me. Her loving look from the Tuesday dawn caresses its pages, and it seems as if her finger beckons as she says to me, "Ruthy, make something out of this."

And that's what I did.

❁　　❁　　❁

I WISH TO EXPRESS my gratitude to *Hakadosh Baruch Hu*, Who rewarded me with the privilege of a dear and special mission, blessing me with the know-how and the capacity of succeeding in transcribing the stories of Rebbetzin Kanievsky *a"h*. Thank You for having granted me the privilege of hearing these pearls of wisdom first-hand to strengthen us all, and of bringing them to publication for the benefit of the public.

I offer thanks to my husband, who encouraged me to publish this vital work and set aside precious time in guiding and providing wise council and true direction, lest something unworthy emerge from under our hands. My thanks to my parents, to the publisher and to all the dear members of my family who supported me all along the way.

Likewise to the Kanievsky family, which encouraged this endeavor, praised the enterprise and then reviewed the manuscript with careful scrutiny. They shared their hope and expectation with me of seeing this in print as quickly as possible.

To Mrs. M. Amrani for her devotion to the Rebbetzin *a"h* and her help early each Tuesday morning.

To my dear friends who offered wise advice as well as practical assistance, even down to the small details.

To the staff of "Dimyon" who were so generous with their time and hearts, and invested so much in designing the beautiful layout of the book.

I would also like to thank Mrs. Sheindel Weinbach and Mrs. Esther Chachamtzedek for their hard work and talent in preparing this English edition.

I pray that the Rebbetzin's words be accepted with grace, and thank Hashem for the privilege of recording her stories.

Ruth Attias

Of Sterling Lineage

R' Yosef Shalom Elyashiv *shlita*

R' Aryeh Levine *ztzvk"l*

REBBETZIN BATSHEVA ESTHER KANIEV-sky *a"h* was born on Rosh Chodesh Adar, 5692 (1932) in Meah Shearim, Jerusalem, to her father, *ylcht"a*, Maran *Hagaon* R' Yosef Shalom Elyashiv *shlita*, and her mother, Sheina Chaya *a"h*, the daughter of *Hagaon* R' Aryeh Levine *ztzvk"l*.

Maran *Harav* Elyashiv was born on the first of Nisan, 5670 (1910), in Lithuania. His maternal grandfather was *Hagaon* R' Shlomo Elyashiv, a famed Kabbalist and author of *Leshem Shvo V'Achlama*, which deals with esoteric kabbalistic matters. His father was the *rav* of Hommel and author of the halachic work *Bikurei Avraham*.

Hagaon R' Aryeh Levine *ztzvk"l* (1885–1969) was the *mashgiach* in Eitz Chaim Yeshiva in Jerusalem. A noted *talmid chacham* and *baal chessed*, he was known by the affectionate nickname of "Father of Prisoners" because of his constant practice of visiting prisoners — especially those condemned by the British to the gallows. He was also known for his visits to the patients in the leper's hospital and to lonely, childless people — all of whom benefited from the sunshine he brought into their wretched lives.

In Kislev of 5712 (1951) the Rebbetzin married Maran R' Shmaryahu Yosef Chaim Kanievsky *shlita*, who was born on the 15th of Teves, 5688 (1927), in Russia. In his youth, Maran studied in Yeshivas Tiferes Zion in Bnei Brak and in Yeshivas Lomza in Petach Tikva.

R' Shmaryahu Yosef Chaim Kanievsky *shlita*

After their marriage, they moved to Shikun Chazon Ish in Bnei Brak. Through her abundant love of Torah, the Rebbetzin endeavored to absolve her husband of every mundane responsibility and burden so that he could devote himself wholly to his study, day and night.

The father of Maran R' Chaim was the Steipler Gaon, Maran R' Yaakov Yisrael Kanievsky *zy"a* (1899–1985), author of a series of works called *Kehillos Yaakov* on Shas. In his youth, he studied in Yeshivas Novhordok, and after immigrating to Eretz Yisrael, served as Rosh Yeshivas of Beis Yosef Novhordok in Bnei Brak.

R' Yaakov Yisrael Kanievsky *zy"a*

R' Chaim Kanievsky *shlita*

Torah

The Grasshopper Who Performed Its Mission

MY HUSBAND, THE RAV, wrote many halachic works. One of them, a very thick volume, was all ready for printing except for one knotty problem holding it up. In one of the chapters, he had written a *halachah* concerning a type of locust, and it was vital for him to know exactly how its wings looked and how they folded. Never having seen a grasshopper in his life, my husband was at a loss to describe it.

He asked me to go to a seminary library and find a picture of a grasshopper in some science book. I went, but couldn't find anything that could help him.

The Rav was very distressed, since exact knowledge of this particular *halachah* would make his *sefer* complete; but without having seen this creature, he could not take it to print.

Just at this very time, at one Shabbos meal, what should appear before his nose but a grasshopper! And the very specie in question! He scrutinized the creature thoroughly, and finally exclaimed, "Now I have my missing information regarding the *halachah*!"

No sooner had he made this declaration than the grasshopper lifted its wings and vanished…

Penny by Penny — For the Sake of Torah Study

MY MOTHER *A"H* LIVED her life, hour by hour, totally concerned that her husband, my father, Maran R' Elyashiv, be able to study Torah in complete peace, without interruptions or disturbances. Thus, for example, my father never had to wait for his meals. At the very moment he entered the kitchen, after *davening* or learning, his meal was ready and the table was prepared.

We were a family of many children, and my grandparents lived with us as well. My mother's supreme concern was, at all times, that my father be able to learn in quiet and serenity.

Erev Pesach is a busy time, with its accompanying tasks of cleaning and then cooking. To be sure, the necessary noise and upheaval would hamper my father's Torah study. Therefore, my mother decided that for the week before Pesach she would send my father to a convalescent home, where he would have the necessary peace and quiet to learn without any disturbances. He remained there until the night of *bedikas chametz*, when he returned home.

My mother financed this week by putting away penny by penny from her daily expenses until she had reached the necessary sum. No one felt it; no one was even aware of it. She was thus able to maintain her supreme goal of enabling her husband to study with a free mind, even during the hectic pre-Pesach week.

Torah Is the Best S'chorah

AN ORPHAN BOY IN Russia had the good fortune of finding refuge with a rich family who adopted him and cared devotedly for all his needs.

One of the children in this family was about to get married. At this stage, the orphan decided it was time for him to leave and go to a yeshiva in northern Russia but realized that he would need warm clothing for the harsh and bitter winter.

He went to his adoptive mother and asked if he could have the *chasan*'s old clothing, since she would surely be outfitting him with a new wardrobe.

The mother was more than glad to comply.

A short while later, the *chasan* came to the orphan bearing a large bundle of clothing. "My mother said that this is for you." The orphan thanked him heartily and they began conversing.

"Listen here," said the *chasan*, "you are a clever fellow with a good head on your shoulders. Why don't you join the family business and work for just two hours a day? That way, you will earn a livelihood and still have plenty of time left for Torah study."

The orphan shook his head vehemently. "I want to devote myself entirely to Torah. I wish to fulfill the *pasuk* '*Shivti b'veis Hashem kol yemei chayai*,' by staying in learning for the rest of my life."

The rich son became inflamed and said, "If you want to live at the expense of others without lifting a finger, you don't deserve this clothing." He took the bundle back and stalked off.

The orphan did not say a word in reply, not even to the *chasan*'s mother. He went off to yeshiva and studied there with utter *mesirus nefesh*, in the freezing Russian weather.

Years passed…

The young man married, joined the family business, and succeeded in amassing great wealth. He became a noted millionaire, flattered and fawned upon by people who loved the glitter of money.

He was once invited to a fundraising dinner and given a place of honor at the dais. As he sat there, he noticed how all eyes were suddenly focused upon the entrance, waiting for some important person to arrive. Someone nearby noted, "A great Rav is about to come. People are waiting to greet him and receive his blessing."

When the esteemed guest, an imposing and venerable figure, showed up, everyone rushed to his side and a long line formed very respectfully, each awaiting his turn to greet the Rav and receive his blessing. The millionaire joined the line, as he also wanted to be blessed by the esteemed Rav.

When his turn came, he suddenly recognized the Rav as the very orphan whom he had basically chased out of his parents' home. He was mortified.

Very humbly, remorsefully and shamefully, he said to the Rav, "I never dreamed that this is what would become of you. I only had your best interest in mind. Please, allow me to make amends and give you a large donation. I truly want the privilege of a share in your Torah!"

The Rav replied, "Unfortunately, now it's not the same situation. I'm no longer a destitute young Torah student. Had you agreed to provide me with warm clothing many years ago when I needed your help, you would have earned a share in my Torah. Sadly, that opportunity is gone now."

That orphan youth who grew in Torah until he became one of the *gedolei hador* was none other than R' Yitzchak Elchanan Spektor *zy"a*.

This deeply moving story shows us the great power of Torah studied through self-sacrifice and deprivation.

Additionally, it demonstrates that some opportunities in life come and go very quickly, and if you miss one, it is gone forever and nothing will bring it back. You can be a millionaire but still be unable to recover that lost opportunity, not for all the money in the world.

The Measure of a Shiur

THURSDAYS ARE THE BUSIEST days in my household. Preparations for Shabbos gain momentum; *challah* dough is prepared, *hafrashas challah* taken, and the house is enveloped in an *erev* Shabbos aura.

In the midst of this frenetic activity, in walks a twelve-year-old girl, just turning bas-mitzvah, seeking my blessing.

I leave everything, bless her very heartily and give her my gift, *Kuntres Chaim VaChessed*, a booklet written by my son-in-law, *Hagaon* R' Yitzchak Kolodetzky, which deals with interpersonal relations, like loving a fellow Jew, receiving people with a pleasant manner, and so on.

As I am penning my personal dedication to the book, in walks another woman, talking on her cell phone to her brother-in-law who tells her that he is scheduled to give a *shiur* in Netanya that day. This weekly *shiur* is usually attended by about thirty people, but for various reasons only three would be coming that day. He asks his sister-in-law to inquire if he should go all the way to Netanya or cancel it altogether.

My husband the Rav was not at home at the time and I didn't know what to tell her.

Suddenly, I opened the book I was about to give to the

bas-mitzvah girl, and on the page in front of me there was a paragraph that mentions that someone had asked the Chazon Ish whether "so-and-so is obligated to deliver a *shiur* that he knows will only be attended by one person."

The Chazon Ish told him, "Go, even if only for one man, because a *Yid* who hasn't heard a *shiur* that day is not the same *Yid* as one who has. It's a difference between heaven and earth."

If that is what the Chazon Ish said, the man on the other end of the line already had his answer…

The Rav's Commitments

MAZEL TOV! MAY IT be in a *gutte sha'ah*! It was a day permeated with emotion, prayer, pressure, hundreds of single minutes culminating in a grand poignant moment — the wedding day of one of our children.

My husband, the Rav, turns to his *mechutan* at one point and murmurs, "How will I ever deal with all my commitments?"

The latter is alarmed. Surely he is referring to financial obligations. What should he do?

He goes over to my husband's *chavrusa*, *Hagaon* R' Dov Berel Weintraub, and tells him very agitatedly that the Rav doesn't know how he can deal with all of his obligations.

R' Dov Berel smiles broadly.

"Why are you smiling?" the *mechutan* asks in surprise.

"It's not like you think and his anxiety has nothing to do with money," he replies. "R' Chaim is fretful about the fact that he still has to fulfill his daily study quota. These are his spiritual obligations, the commitments which he has to meet every day. But now, at the wedding, he cannot pick himself up in the middle and go off to some quiet corner to learn and he is wondering how he will manage..."

Love for Torah

MY SISTER LEAH *A"H,* deceased wife of my brother-in-law *Hagaon* R' Ezriel Auerbach *ylcht"a,* was a real *tzadekes.* A love for Torah burned deeply in her bones and her *yiras Shamayim* was an inseparable part of her being, a guiding light for all her actions.

My sister lived in Bayit Vegan for sixteen years, but devotedly paid a visit to our father, Maran R' Elyashiv, every single day to serve him in every way possible so that he could continue studying uninterruptedly. She even decided to take a leave of absence from her teaching position in order to devote herself to *kibbud av,* which was so very important to her.

Each summer, she would take our parents into her home, where they could enjoy peace and quiet, away from their daily bustle and cares. Again, her primary consideration was that our father be able to study undisturbed.

When she passed away — even before she was laid to rest — my father asked that a special garment be brought to him, the garment he wore when he was honored as *sandak* at a *bris.* He put in on and said, "I want to wear this garment, the most special one I possess, so that I can tear *kriyah* on it over my dear daughter who was also so special."

"Each of us who enables her husband to learn Torah without distractions should be aware that when she arrives at the World of Truth, she will merit sitting next to her husband, and that all of his Torah [acquisition] will also be credited to her."

(From the words of Rebbetzin Kanievsky)

Hagaon R. Chaim Kanievsky with his sons during the Rebbetzin's shivah

By What Merit?

How do women merit a portion
in Olam HaBa?
(Berachos 13a)

"I Compare You to the Horse of Pharaoh's Chariot"

I AM ACCUSTOMED TO telling over words of Torah and encouragement to my dear visitors. I want them to realize and understand how fortunate they are and how good is their lot to be privileged to toil so that their husbands can study Torah with a free mind.

The song which the Jewish women sang at the Red Sea begins with "And Miriam answered them and said... 'A horse and its rider were flung into the sea.'" Why does it say that she answered them? Did anyone ask her a question? If so, what is the question and what is the answer?

It can be explained thus: The Jewish women were saddened and pained when they heard that only the menfolk had been given the privilege of learning Torah. Why should only they sit and learn and receive reward for every minute? What would become of the women?

Miriam answered them, "A horse and its rider were flung into the sea."

The horse serves its rider by bringing him to his destination. This is why the horses of Egypt were punished alongside their masters.

From here, Miriam concluded that Jewish women, their

husbands' helpmates, would also receive reward for the Torah that their husbands studied.

Without the wives, the men would not be able to study with the same dedication and peace of mind.

If the women are truly so instrumental in helping their husbands learn, then, when they come to the World of Truth, the wives will sit alongside their mates and share the merit that the husbands accumulated over their many years of study. Indeed, they made it possible.

This, then, is how the women will gain the merit of Torah study.

Fortunate is the woman who merits it!

The Wedding Ring

THERE WAS ONCE A young man who yearned to devote his whole life purely to Torah study.

When he reached marriageable age, he made this goal very clear to all candidates: Even when the family grew and there were many children, he would want to continue learning and not even assume a Torah-related position which would rob him of precious study time.

He found a young girl who rose to the challenge and agreed to this condition. After their marriage, the young bride supported them while he immersed himself in study. The years passed and the family grew. By the time the couple had ten children, the financial situation was extremely difficult and the woman finally approached her husband and suggested, "Perhaps the time has come for you to take a job related to Torah. Maybe you can become a *maggid shiur* in some yeshiva?"

"My dear wife," he said, "we came to an agreement before we got married that I would devote myself to pure study for the rest of my days. Why should we put an end to all these years of self-sacrifice for Torah by my taking a job?"

The wife nodded her head; her husband was right and she accepted his decision but asked his permission to sell the diamond ring she had received from him. He agreed.

She took the ring to a jeweler.

"You got this ring as a gift from your husband? How can you sell it?" he asked in shock.

She explained that she wanted her husband to "stay in learning" and this was the only way to make it possible. The jeweler was so moved by her words that he said, "I have a brother who is a diamond expert. Go to him and he will appraise the ring for you at its true value." She took the address and went off to the other dealer.

She gave him the ring to examine, without saying anything. But the brother was altogether bewildered. "I am no diamond expert," he exclaimed. "Why in the world did my brother send you to me? This is very strange."

The woman began explaining why she was selling the ring.

Deeply moved, he said to her, "I am not a diamond dealer but I *am* a wealthy businessman and I am very touched to hear of such devotion, such *mesirus nefesh* for Torah. I want a share; I am willing to support you from now on so that your husband, who is a diamond, can continue studying without any financial burden, just as he wishes!"

Tears Turned to Pearls

WHEN THE MAHARAM LUBLIN, *Hagaon* R' Meir Shapira, was a little boy, his mother hired a *melamed* to teach him. She chose the best one she could find. He took a high fee, which she really couldn't afford, but this did not stop her from getting the very best for her Meir'ke. She sold all of her jewelry to pay the tuition.

Each morning, she would sit on the side and listen to Meir's clear childish voice repeating the *gemara* after the Rebbe. It was sweet music to her ears.

One morning, the *melamed* did not show up. The mother sat and waited, crying over the delay. She waited and cried, waited and cried all the while. "Why are you so distressed?" little Meir asked his mother. "What's so terrible if I miss one day? I can learn again tomorrow!"

"No, my son," said the mother, wiping away another tear. "A day gone is a day lost forever. It will never return! It's a terrible pity for every moment not used for learning." And her tears started rolling down her cheeks again.

Those tears never dried. They continued to fall [figuratively] each day anew, filtering deep into the boy's *neshamah*, to remain there forevermore. Those were tears that told the story of a mother who sacrificed all she had so that her only son could learn. She never bought anything for herself — only for Meir'ke. The tears she shed tell of the importance of every moment devoted to Torah study.

The boy grew to eventually become the famed Maharam Shapira of Lublin, founder of Yeshivas Chachmei Lublin and the initiator of the idea of the Daf HaYomi regimen and its instigator as a worldwide movement.

Wherever there are Jews, in Eretz Yisrael and abroad, they are united by the study of the same page of *gemara*, the Daf HaYomi, and their hearts are drawn closer together. Every seven-and-half years, the entire Jewish world celebrates the *Siyum HaShas*, having completed the entire study of the Talmud, a day at a time, a *daf* a day.

Many years passed since that day of tears. The Maharam's mother had long since passed away, but one night, she appeared to a friend in a dream, a figure bathed in radiance, a diamond-studded crown upon her head.

"Would you believe it?" she whispered in the dream. "Every day when the world studies yet another page of *gemara*, another diamond is set into my crown. And all this is in the merit of my son, R' Meir, and in the merit of those tears I shed for him. It is in the reward for the jewels I sold so that Meir could learn Torah."

A Blessing on Her Wedding Day

MANY *KALLOS* COME TO me early on the morning of their wedding day to receive a blessing on this momentous occasion in their lives. One such *kallah* appeared at 6:00 A.M., very emotional, eager to be blessed.

I told the future bride the fascinating story about the diamond ring and the devotion of a couple with ten children to Torah — how the wife was prepared to sell the gift she had gotten on her wedding day and which was so precious to her so that her husband could continue studying Torah.

I highlighted the tremendous, immediate *siyata diShmaya* they merited through the rich man who was so impressed with her sacrifice that he promised to support the family in the future so that, indeed, the husband could devote himself purely to Torah.

My purpose was to emphasize to this *kallah* the importance of her husband's study under all circumstances.

"You should know," I said, "that Hashem sends His special *siyata diShmaya* to every home where there is a genuine love and commitment to the husband's Torah study — pure and undisturbed."

I tell all the *kallos* the importance of giving way to the

husband's will, to be *mevater*, to sustain him with compliments, encouragement and show the proper respect for one who is devoted to Torah study. It really helps so much…

I added that my mother was such a woman, one who was privileged to do everything she possibly could — and always through love and joy.

Each and every one of us who does this should know that when she comes to the World of Truth, she will merit to sit next to her husband, and that all of his Torah acquisition will be hers, as well, to share.

The Role of a Rebbetzin

I ALWAYS SAY: "HOW can a Rav grow to great heights if he is so beset by the inevitable disturbances and interruptions that are a necessary part of his position? It is indeed extremely difficult..."

If, however, his wife fulfills her role as a Rebbetzin, through devotion and with joy, deflecting disruptions, then he can truly grow. He will be able to study Torah and also fulfill his obligation and mission as a Rav and even produce many *sefarim*. In other words, behind each Rav is a devoted Rebbetzin.

The woman's role is to enable her husband to learn without disturbances, in peace and quiet. This is her mission in this world; it is an obligation that is simultaneously a privilege!

By her actively shielding her husband from disruptions, by not troubling him with various requests, while at the same time encouraging and praising him, creating the proper atmosphere conducive to study, she is freeing him of all obstacles and barriers so that he can reach truly great spiritual heights — and she is also rising, together with him.

The Role of a Jewish Mother

A JEWISH MOTHER MUST be aware that she plays a tremendous role in her children's education. "*Shema b'ni...* Hearken my son to your father's *mussar* and do not reject your mother's teachings."

A father studies with his sons, but a mother is the one who is in the home and who serves as the personal example and role model for proper behavior, deference (*vitur*), concentration in prayer, and love and respect for Torah and *mitzvos*.

Young children observe their mother all the time; they see what she does, how she does it, and they internalize what is truly important to her. That which they see becomes their aspiration and the object of emulation in their lives.

A mother must fulfill the role of "*Ima,*" with all the warmth and feeling of a *Yiddishe* Mama. She must teach her children how to make a *berachah* with *kavanah*, impress upon them the importance of answering "*Amen*" and demonstrate to them the affection and respect she has for the Torah. She must show them in practice how she waits longingly for them to return from *cheder* with a loving smile.

Special Mesirus Nefesh for the Rav's Sleep

MY FATHER, MARAN HARAV Elyashiv, sleeps for a very short time each night — only about three hours — after which he gets up and resumes his Torah study. Moreover, he is a very light sleeper and is easily awakened.

During the last days of my mother's life, she lay virtually on her deathbed, suffering from diseased lungs which caused her spells of wracking coughing. She was already so weak that she couldn't stand on her feet.

The doctors in the hospital declared that there was nothing more that they could do for her, and since her days were numbered, she should return home — for her own sake.

My mother came home and lay in bed, unable to move. Her grandsons took turns staying the night with her so that if she needed anything, they would be on hand.

Late one night, when the grandson "on duty" went in to check on his grandmother, he was alarmed to find that her bed was empty!

"Where could Savta have gone?" he murmured in fear. She was so ill that she couldn't get out of bed without help. He went looking for her everywhere in the house, but she was nowhere to be found. He finally went out onto the porch, and there she was, doubled over, trying desperately to suppress a coughing spell.

"Savta! What are you doing here?" he asked. "How did you ever succeed in getting out of bed and coming here? You can't even walk a step by yourself!"

The *tzadekes* took a deep breath and replied, "The Rav's sleep is so sensitive that he wakes up from every noise. His sleep is so short to begin with, and so necessary, that I didn't want to disturb it with my coughing. He needs to wake up refreshed for the long day's study and *avodas Hashem* still ahead of him."

She paused to gather strength, then continued, "I lay in bed and suddenly felt a coughing spell coming on. Fearing that it would wake the Rav up, I somehow got out of bed and crawled on all fours, very slowly, until I reached the porch. Only then did I allow myself to cough."

She remained there until the coughing subsided and only then would she allow herself to be helped back to her bed.

She passed away the following day…

Here, in the Lederman shul, was the Rebbetzin's special place where she davened; and here is the siddur from which she prayed three times a day, pleading for all of Klal Yisrael.

Prayer

Ein Od Milvado

MANY WOMEN COME TO me with their various ills and complaints. At times, they have a specific request to ask, at others, it is something pressing on their hearts. What do I invariably tell them all? "Declare with all your heart and soul what R' Chaim Volozhiner taught us to say fervently at all times, '*Hashem Hu haElokim; ein od Milvado* — Hashem is G-d; there is none besides Him.'"

One must know and believe that Hashem never does something "bad." If a person has sinned and is beset by suffering or hardship, it is in order to purify him. It is up to him to examine his deeds to see if he has sinned, and to find a way to rectify what he has done wrong.

Actually, a person should examine himself all the time and introspect. He should ask himself how s/he can improve himself and in what areas s/he can advance: *tzniyus*, guarding one's speech, Shabbos and so on. The underlying principle to remember is that Hashem doesn't punish. He loves us all and we are completely in His benevolent hands. The reality is simply: "*Ein od Milvado* — there is none besides Him."

A Jew once came to me with a woeful tale of a very complicated problem with the tax court. He was extremely apprehensive. I gave him my universal remedy: to declare with all his heart and with full *kavanah*: "*Hashem Hu haElokim; ein od Milvado.*"

He did just that.

Incredibly, his file was lost and his case was dismissed. He emerged completely innocent!

And Say "Amen"

A *TZADDIK* BY THE name of Rav Horowitz was a steady congregant of the Lederman shul. Shortly after he passed away, he appeared to a friend in a dream and told him that the Jews in our generation take answering "*Amen*" too lightly. This is criticized in Heaven.

From the time I heard that, I resolved, *bli neder*, to introduce something new at the Lederman shul and maintain it. Early each morning, when women gather in the women's section even before the *davening* begins, I made it a practice of having each woman in turn recite the *birchos hashachar* out loud, to which the others would answer "*Amen*." This way, we would all gain many mitzvos. This worthy practice has become a regular daily routine.

When *Hagaon* R' Yehuda Leib Shteinman *shlita* heard about this practice from his grandson, who is also my grandson, he told him a very stirring story about R' Chaim Volozhiner who once resolved not to take any food or drink into his mouth unless there was someone in the vicinity to answer "*Amen*" to his blessing.

One time, he felt a terrible thirst and longed for a drink. There was no one about at the moment, so he refused to drink. He waited and waited, but no one came.

His thirst increased, until he was on the verge of fainting; but a resolution is a resolution, and he would not break his word.

Then, suddenly and unexpectedly, one of this *talmidim* appeared. R' Chaim took advantage of the moment, made a *berachah* and waited for the *talmid* to answer "*Amen*" before he took the long-awaited reviving drink.

The next day, R' Chaim approached that *talmid* and thanked him for enabling him to fulfill his resolution the previous day.

"To thank me? But I didn't even see the Rav yesterday!"

R' Chaim could only conclude that Hashem had sent Eliyahu haNavi especially to answer "*Amen*" so that his blessing could be complete.

In the Merit of Waiting to Answer "Amen"

A YOUNG GIRL CAME to me one time. Her mother had passed away and she wanted to do something *le'iluy nishmasah*, for the benefit of her departed soul. She took upon herself not to taste anything unless someone was around to answer "*Amen*" to her *berachah*.

My husband had his reservations and said to me, "She took upon herself something very difficult indeed!"

The girl had told me that one night she had felt an extreme hunger, an intense desire to eat something, but everyone in the house was already asleep and she didn't want to wake anyone. She was at a loss.

All she could do was wait. And she waited for a long time, but nothing happened.

She had no choice but to go to sleep very, very hungry.

Her act of self-sacrifice apparently made a tremendous impression in Heaven. That night, she told me, her departed mother appeared to her in a dream and said, "I want you to know that in the merit of your exceptional deed which shook the Heavens, your dear classmate, who has been diagnosed with a terrible disease, will recover."

The young girl awoke the next morning very bewildered.

She hadn't even known that her friend was ill, but in any event, she went and told her about her dream.

She learned that her friend did, in fact, have the dreaded disease, but had kept it a closely guarded secret. No one in their class knew about it.

"I want you to know that although you are sick right now, I'm positive that you will recover," she told her. "In my dream, my mother promised that this would truly happen."

Not long after that, the friend was given a clean bill of health from her doctor and no signs remained of the dreaded sickness.

When R' Aharon Yehudah Leib Shteinman heard the story, he said that he also wanted to institute the practice of replying "*Amen*" to the morning *berachos* in his shul, Divrei Shir. He would ask people to come a bit earlier so that they could make the rounds of the *berachos*, and let each person say them in turn and have his *berachos* completed with the "*Amen*" of the fellow *mispalelim* in the shul.

The Power of Tehillim

MY FOUR-YEAR-OLD GRANDDAUGHTER ONCE heard an ambulance siren wailing.

She looked outside the window and saw her neighbor being carried out on a stretcher. On the spot, she remained standing and recited the *perek, 'Lamnatzei'ach...'*

The neighbor was released from the hospital on the following day — which was totally unexpected for her condition. I am convinced that this happened in the merit of the little girl's *perek Tehillim*.

When my granddaughter was asked how she had come to know it by heart, she said that her kindergarten teacher had taught it to the girls in *gan*.

The Power of Prayer

I ONCE HEARD A chilling story from a woman who came to me. "My twelve-year-old daughter developed a tumor on her brain stem which was causing spells of unconsciousness. Due to its size and location, the doctors told her that it was inoperable and that there was nothing they could do for her."

Weeping and desperate, she came to me to ask if there was anything *she* could do.

"Do you keep Shabbos?" I asked her.

"Yes," she answered.

"Do you *daven*?" I asked.

"I don't have the time," she said. "I have small children who keep me very busy and I can't find time to *daven*."

"Try to say at least one prayer from a *siddur*, once a day, with all your heart and full concentration," I advised her.

The mother agreed to do this — to say one prayer very earnestly from a *siddur*, and then she turned to go. Before she left, I asked her to keep me posted on her daughter's condition. A few days later, a small boy came to me, the girl's brother, and said that his sister was feeling much better. She was fainting less often and the improvement was very noticeable.

Her doctors also noted the change, and the mother told them what I had advised.

Seeing that the condition was so much better, they decided to risk surgery, but they wanted it to be performed abroad, in a European hospital which had a world famous surgeon on its staff. He had achieved great success in delicate operations of this kind.

A date was set and arrangements were made. As the appointed day neared, the patient continued to improve.

The family was in a dilemma. Should they travel to Europe as planned or cancel the whole thing?

They came to me again and I said to them, "The full *yeshuah* will come when the girl is abroad."

The mother was unable to accompany the girl because she had given birth in the meantime, so the father went, together with a married son. They took along all the C.T. scans and test results, as well as the doctors' recommendations for emergency surgery.

They came to the famous surgeon and showed him the girl's medical file. He examined the patient, studied the C.T. scan and set a date for the operation.

The day arrived. The girl was hospitalized in advance and prepared for surgery, having fasted beforehand. All was ready for the anesthesiologist to administer the anesthesia, which would put her to sleep for the next twelve hours.

A moment before they began, the surgeon suddenly decided, without any logical explanation, to delay the procedure. "In this case, administering the anesthesia itself is somewhat risky. I want to do another C.T. on the girl before we proceed to see if we really need to put her to sleep for so long."

They took a new C.T. scan, and everyone waited impatiently for the results. When the scan came back, it was unbelievable — a miracle! All that remained from the tumor was a small spot on the film. The tumor was gone!

The surgeon couldn't believe it. There must have been a mistake. He studied the film again and again. Finally, he called off the surgery and said that he wished to wait two weeks to see what would happen. Would another C.T. verify the miracle?

Messengers of the family came to me to tell me of the sudden change of plans. They asked if the girl should remain abroad for two weeks to perform the test or return to Israel and do it here.

"The *yeshuah* has already come," I told them. "They can come home."

The girl, her father and her brother returned to Israel.

Two weeks later, her attending physician sent her for another C.T. scan. Not only had the tumor disappeared, but even the black spot was no longer there.

This story moves me anew each time I think of it. See how great is the power of prayer with *kavanah*. I hereby make a special heartfelt plea to each and every one of us: Please, do your utmost to *daven* at least once a day — at least one prayer — from a *siddur* and with great *kavanah!*

Every erev Shabbos someone laid out a special white covering over the shelf in the corner of the Lederman shul where Rebbetzin Kanievsky always davened.

Shabbos Kodesh

The Gift of Shabbos

I COULD HEAR THE sobs already from the stairs, intensifying as the woman approached. When she entered the house, tears were streaming down her face, and her sobbing had turned into a heart-piercing wail.

"I have only one daughter," she finally told me, amidst her weeping. "She was recently involved in a terrible car accident, which left her with a severe head injury. She is still in the hospital, lying in a coma."

She continued speaking between pitiful sobs. "I spend long hours by her bedside each day, doing whatever I can for her. I talk to her and I cry. I talk to her some more and cry my heart out. What is going to be with the poor child? What can I do to help her?

"The doctors tell me that there is no hope for her. I refuse to believe them. I shout and cry that surely there must be a chance she will recover. They say her condition is so grave that she probably won't last much longer."

"Do you keep Shabbos?" I asked the women.

"I sometimes light candles…" she told me, apologetically.

I assumed a very cheerful, hopeful expression and said gently, "You really should begin keeping Shabbos. In our

Friday night prayers we say, 'Let us go to greet the Shabbos [Queen] for she is the source of blessing.' Shabbos is a conduit for channeling a wealth of blessings and *yeshuos* for everyone who observes it properly. I bless you that if you keep Shabbos as it should be kept, Shabbos will, in turn, watch over your daughter."

For someone not used to the restrictions of Shabbos, it was a very difficult decision, but the woman was willing to commit herself to keeping it with all her heart.

After only one week, she came again to me. Instead of the tears and sobs of the first time, now she was full of smiles. She was glowing with happiness.

"My daughter came out of the coma! She woke up!" she said. Now she was crying tears of joy. "I kept Shabbos properly and my daughter came to life!"

This woman received a beautiful gift from the Shabbos Queen — her daughter.

A Non-Jew Who Kept Shabbos

A DISTINGUISHED PERSON, HEAD of a seminary for *baalos te-shuvah*, came to my father, Rav Elyashiv, to discuss a strange condition that affected one of his students.

It concerned a *baalas teshuvah*, a refined and worthy young woman who truly made every effort to keep the *mitzvos* properly to the best of her ability.

There was one big problem in her life: Ever since she had become observant, she would keep Shabbos correctly — that is, until late afternoon. Just before Shabbos would end, she would feel a fierce, inexplicable desire to smoke. She knew very well that it was forbidden but the urge would be so strong, so gripping, that it would send shivers through her entire body. She would tremble so severely that she would actually lose consciousness and her life would be in danger.

The only thing that would help, that would save her, was smoking one cigarette. After this, she would feel completely revived and back to normal.

She had been examined by medical specialists, but they couldn't find anything wrong with her. Nor could they explain how smoking one cigarette could bring such relief from her dangerous condition. She went to a number of *rabbanim* who all ruled that since the matter was actually life threatening, she would be allowed to smoke one cigarette. "*Pikuach nefesh* overrules Shabbos," they decided.

It pained her very much but she had no choice — yet she did not give up on finding a better solution.

One day, someone suggested that her case be brought before Rav Elyashiv. Perhaps he would be able to solve the riddle and help this poor woman.

My father listened to the story and then asked, "Are you sure that this woman is really Jewish? Perhaps she is a gentile by birth? If so, then she is not permitted to keep Shabbos. The *halachah* determines that a gentile who keeps Shabbos is punishable by death. She may think that she is really Jewish but I advise that you check it out thoroughly."

The woman examined her roots and discovered that indeed, she was not a kosher Jew after all. Her mother had not been Jewish but had only pretended to be. Our *baalas teshuvah* had no idea that she wasn't really Jewish.

Heaven had prevented her from keeping Shabbos properly so that she wouldn't be liable the punishment of death. Now that she knew the truth, the good woman went to a *beis din* and converted according to *halachah*.

An amazing thing happened: As soon as she had undergone the conversion, she was freed from her terrible urge to smoke on Shabbos and no longer suffered the strange fainting spells. Gone were the tremors that had shaken her body. Now she was able to keep Shabbos properly from beginning to end.

כניסה
לעזרת נשים
ולאולם שמחות
לנשים בלבד

Here, near the gate, is where Rebbetzin Kanievsky used to stand, early each morning after davening vasikin. Here is where she would shower her blessings, utter comforting words and pour out her love to the dozens of women who came from near and far.

Character Traits

R' Shlomo Zalman and the Lone Tree

TWO FRUIT TREES GREW in the yard of *Hagaon* R' Shlomo Zalman Auerbach *zy"a*. Each year, in the month of Nisan, when they were in bloom, *rabbanim* would come to say *birkas ha'ilanos* over them, since it is preferable to recite this blessing over two trees rather than over one.

A sizeable gathering came all at one time for the annual event but at one point, the *rabbanim* noticed that R' Shlomo Zalman had slipped away and was not saying the *berachah* along with the others. They watched him walk out of the courtyard and saw him go over to a tree growing by itself in the yard of a woman who lived not far away. He stood in front of this single tree and said the *berachah* over it.

When he returned, the *rabbanim* asked him, "Why don't you recite *birkas ha'ilanos* over your own two trees along with the rest of us? Isn't that the preferred way?"

"The woman in that other yard once told me that she tended and nurtured her tree throughout the year especially so that I should come and recite the blessing over it in Nisan," he replied. How can I ignore her great effort and disappoint her by reciting it in my own yard?"

Born Anew

WHEN I WAS RECEIVING the public one time, I suddenly felt extremely weak and tired, almost about to faint. I wanted to know how many more women were still waiting outside to see me. I noticed a girl of about eleven among the group and asked her why she hadn't come in.

"I have a very personal request to make of the Rebbe-tzin," she replied.

I took her to an inner room where we could have privacy. As soon as the door was closed behind us, the girl burst into tears.

"Everything is going wrong in my life," she sobbed. "I have no friends; school is so hard, and I fail almost every test; and at home, no one even cares about me."

Her tears pierced my heart. She looked so miserable, so pitiful, that soon I was crying along with her. I asked her what grade she was in and which school she attended. It turned out that I had a granddaughter in her very class. I told her that she would be happy to help her.

I was unable to sleep that entire night. The sorrowful figure stood before me all the time. Early the next morning, I called my granddaughter and told her about her unhappy classmate and how important it was for her to befriend and help her.

"Don't worry, Savta," she reassured me. "I'll do whatever I can for her."

My granddaughter, may she be well, took the project upon herself with all her heart. She began studying with the girl and helped integrate her into the social structure of the class, while I followed with great interest and encouragement. The progress was phenomenal. The girl's test scores began to rise, from in the sixties to the seventies, and then in the eighties — and she even scored an occasional one hundred.

To be sure, no one was aware of the special attention and encouragement she was getting — except for my granddaughter and me.

One day, the girl's mother, who was not aware of what was going on behind the scenes, came to me. She spoke very emotionally and said, "I am so grateful to Hashem for His great kindness. I have a daughter who was a social misfit and a failure in her studies. I didn't know what to do with her. She used to sit around the house all alone, moping. She didn't want to go to school anymore and just locked herself up in her room and lay on her bed, staring at the ceiling.

"Then, all of a sudden, for no apparent reason, there was an amazing transformation, a complete about-face. She is not the same child anymore. She has friends, is doing very well in school, does her homework willingly and is very happy. Her teacher says that she has improved so much that she is one of the better students in the class."

There is an important lesson to be learned here. Any girl

can take a weaker student under her wing, befriend her, help her with her schoolwork and include her in social activities. One must look around to see who needs extra attention, some encouragement and help.

It is so important to take an interest in the other girls in your class or women in your neighborhood, and to smile at everyone and be friendly. You can build entire worlds in this way.

A Match – Thanks to Giving Way

IT WAS VACATION TIME, towards the end of summer. People were searching for ways to escape the stifling heat of the city. The A's, a family with ten children, were also seeking relief from the heat and had arranged to rent a vacation apartment in Tzefas, up north, high in the mountains.

The A's packed their numerous bundles, stuffed clothing into suitcases and hired a van. They were off, heading for the cool northern part of the country.

When they arrived, they discovered to their great dismay that another family had already made itself at home in the apartment which they, too, had reserved for themselves.

There had been a terrible mistake, and the one apartment had been promised to two families.

Each family claimed the right to the apartment. The one which had come first said it was rightfully theirs, while the A's said that they had also been promised the apartment. In the end, the A's bowed gracefully out and decided to return to the steaming heat of their apartment in the central part of the country.

As disappointed as they were, the parents were able to

make peace with the situation. Not so the children, who had pinned high hopes on this vacation. They were so saddened by the change of plans that the parents spontaneously decided to give them a special trip on the way home: a visit to the Kosel and a tour of the Old City.

On the way there, they stopped off to *daven minchah* at a major yeshiva. The oldest son, an unmarried young man of twenty-five, began *davening Shemoneh Esrei* with deep fervor and concentration.

The Rosh Yeshiva was in the *beis medrash* at time and couldn't help being impressed by the young man. There was something so pure and beautiful about the way he prayed that the Rosh Yeshiva was beside himself with admiration.

"This is the kind of young man I want for my daughter," he thought, his high regard increasing all the while.

He made inquiries about the young visitor and matters developed to the point that the young man eventually became the son-in-law of that Rosh Yeshiva.

This would not have happened had the family remained in Tzefas; it was because of their generous "surrender" of the vacation apartment, their yielding to the other family, that the *shidduch* came about. This teaches us the power of yielding (*vitur*) — one never loses by doing so.

Not to Offend a Jewish Daughter

I HAVE TWO DARLING five-year-old granddaughters who are in kindergarten.

These two cousins are great friends and live in the same city but do not attend the same *gan*. While they regretted this very much, they hoped that when they got to first grade, they would be in the same school, the same class, and even sit on the same bench.

They used to count the days in the year until they would be in first grade, when they would be close together. It was so important to them that each time they came to visit, they reminded me, "Savta, next year we're going to sit right next to each other."

They were always chattering about how things would be when they got to school. The closer the time came, the more excited they became.

Then, finally, the first day of school arrived. It was very exciting, with a very festive welcoming program. When one of the granddaughters came to me afterwards, I asked her, "So who are you sitting next to?" although I already knew the answer. Hadn't the two dreamt about it for a whole year?

My granddaughter surprised me. She wasn't sitting next to her cousin at all, but next to a different girl.

"What happened?" I asked.

She told me, in the sweetest, childlike manner, "When I went into the classroom, a girl came over and asked if she could sit next to me. What could I say to her? No? She would have been terribly hurt. So I smiled at her and said, 'Yes, of course!'"

I was amazed at a girl who had just turned six and her power of resilience, her ability to yield, to give up a sweet dream, the anticipation of an entire year — in order not to hurt another person's feelings.

Yehonasan

A BABY BOY IS born in the family. What should they name him? The parents considered giving the name Yehonasan, since this had been the name of a beloved grandfather who had been an upright *tzaddik*.

Right before the *bris,* the couple went to their *rav* for his blessing, and to tell him the name they had chosen for their son. To their surprise, he said, "Don't call the baby by that name, even though you want to honor the grandfather who had been a *tzaddik.*"

Why?

In the building where this couple lived, there was a woman whose young son had died in childhood. His name had been Yehonasan. "Try to project yourself into the future. If you called your son Yehonasan, then each time he was playing outside and you wanted him to come home to eat or to run an errand, you would call his name out loud. And each time, that bereaved mother would be reminded of her departed son and the wound would be reopened anew."

The parents realized that it was a delicate issue and they chose another name for their son.

How sensitive and far thinking that rabbi was! How

important it is for us, too, to be attuned to other people's issues, to things that can cause them pain — even if only in the future. This is an outlook and sensitivity which we should all acquire.

Yielding Saves Lives

THE BOY WAS BESIDE himself with excited anticipation. *Parshas Yisro* was going to be his bar-mitzvah Shabbos. He would be called up to the Torah reading and would even be allowed to *lein* the whole *parshah* himself, as was the custom in his shul.

He practiced for this — weeks upon weeks — until he knew it perfectly, letter by letter, and felt fully prepared and confident. It would be his big day.

His father had met with the *gabbai* long before to make sure he reserved the date for them. Then he had reminded him several more times to keep that Shabbos free for the bar mitzvah, and each time the *gabbai* had confirmed it. "Yes, don't worry; that's *your* Shabbos."

The big day finally arrived. The boy came to shul on Shabbos morning, all excited. His mother brought huge bags of nuts and candies, as well as other refreshments, but the boy had his mind on the Torah reading for which he had prepared so long and well.

Suddenly, he couldn't help noticing another boy his age, wearing a hat and suit, his family loaded down with refreshments as well. In a flash, he understood that this was another bar-mitzvah boy, one who planned on reading the *parshah* just as he had.

How could it be? How could this have happened?

He made a quick calculation and realized that one of them would have to give way to the other. Both of them couldn't read from the Torah at the same time! One of them would read and the other would have to stand by... and listen.

The battle raged fiercely inside him. The *yetzer tov* and the *yetzer hara* were fighting it out, each one arguing vehemently that it was right. As expected, one of them won.

The first bar-mitzvah boy went quietly over to the *gabbai* and stated that he was bowing out and letting the other boy have the honor of reading the Torah.

He had decided that he would be the one to yield and give way.

It hadn't been an easy decision. Not in the least!

A year passed and *Parshas Yisro* came around once again. Tears came to the young boy's eyes when he remembered how he hadn't read the *parshah* for which he had practiced so hard. The memory still pained him deeply even though he did not regret his noble deed. Still, he couldn't help wondering why things had to happen that way...

Four years passed and he was now a youth of seventeen. His mother became very ill and was hospitalized. Things did not look good. The doctors went so far as to say that her days were numbered. The son remained dutifully by his sick mother's bedside, seeing her slipping slowly away from this world and feeling very helpless.

On a different floor in the same hospital, my father, Maran Rav Elyashiv, was also hospitalized. He hadn't been feeling well and the doctors had advised that he stay over Shabbos to be under medical supervision.

As soon as he knew that he would have to be hospitalized over Shabbos, my father asked that a *mehudar sefer Torah* be brought to him for the Shabbos reading. He also asked that they arrange for an expert *baal korei* to come and *lein*. Everything seemed to fall right into place.

Shabbos arrived, and with it, a special *minyan* to *daven* with my father. The seventeen-year-old boy joined it at night.

The next morning, the group *davened Shacharis*. When the time came to read from the Torah, they discovered that they didn't have a *baal korei* after all. They had forgotten to arrange for one and no one was prepared or familiar enough with the *parshah* to be able to read it — especially for Rav Elyashiv, who was a perfectionist!

They asked around. Was there anyone competent who could volunteer? Suddenly, a young boy stepped forward and offered his services. "I know the *parshah* almost backwards and forwards," he said. "It's my bar-mitzvah *parshah*."

The *minyan* had no choice and agreed to let the boy *lein*. He did a masterful job, reading precisely and correctly, to everyone's amazement.

My father is very exacting and particular about reading from the Torah, making sure that every letter and vowel is pronounced correctly. He followed the *leining* with admiration; it was flawless. He was overjoyed that Heaven had sent him such a wonderful *baal korei* and inquired about the boy who had done such a beautiful job.

The young boy went over to him and explained that it had been his bar mitzvah *parshah* which he had studied long and hard. He went on to tell Rav Elyashiv how he had forfeited actually reading from the Torah on his bar mitz-vah, and that this was the first time he had done so. Rav Elyashiv asked him what he was doing in the hospital and he explained that his mother was very ill and had been told that she only had a few days to live.

My father was under the care of a famous specialist. He asked the doctor to examine the sick woman very thor-oughly to see that if her life could be saved.

When the specialist examined the patient, he realized that she had been getting the wrong treatment all along. The medication was immediately stopped and a different one was given to her.

Today that woman is alive and healthy; may she con-tinue to enjoy many more years of good health and *nachas* from her son.

Her recovery came about all because of an amazing *vitur*, a submission and yielding of way...

A Mutual Capitulation

ON THE DAY OF his *chasunah*, my grandfather, *Hagaon* R' Aryeh Levine *ztzvk"l*, said to his *kallah*: "It is the accepted custom for a *chasan* to give his new bride a gift on their wedding day. I would also like to do that, but I don't have any money. However, I do have something to offer. I have decided that the biggest gift I can give you is *vitur*, submission and yielding, for the rest of your life."

My grandmother was touched to the point of tears and said, "That very gift shall also be my gift to you. Submission and yielding to you for the rest of our married life."

No wonder then that these two giants of spirit were rewarded with a giant in Torah, a *gaon* and *tzaddik* who married their daughter: my father, Maran *Hagaon* R' Yosef Shalom Elyashiv *shlita*.

Vitur, yielding to others, is truly the key to many wonderful blessings!

So That Her Friend Wouldn't Be Pained

MY FOUR-YEAR-OLD GRANDDAUGHTER IS a very exceptional, wonderful child.

After the tragic death of *Hagaon* R' Moshe Geffen *zt"l*, *Ra"m* in Yeshivas Chadera, we discussed the painful accident in our home in the presence of our granddaughter. She listened to the adult conversation and suddenly exclaimed: "Savta, do you know that the granddaughter of R' Geffen is in my kindergarten?"

"Really?" I said. "Did you talk to her about her grandfather?"

"Oh, no!" she exclaimed. "How could I? Maybe no one told her, and she doesn't even know that he isn't alive anymore? If she found out from me, she would be so upset!"

This is the pot in which Rebbetzin Kanievsky cooked her gefilte fish in huge quantities, every week, distributing it lovingly and joyfully to whomever wanted. She would always serve herself last...

Tzedakah and Chessed

Tzedakah Saves from Death

THE OLD CITY. JERUSALEM of a century ago. The city of my grandfather, *Hagaon Hatzaddik* R' Aryeh Levine *ztzvk"l*, my *tzadekes* grandmother, and their blessed family.

It was a time of great poverty, when people had very little, and running water was a symbol of wealth. Most people drew their water from wells and stored it in vessels in their homes. This was how my grandparents lived, as well.

One day, my grandmother realized she was out of some vital staples for her family, and she needed to slip out for a brief moment down to the *makolet*. Her infant daughter was asleep on the bed in what she was sure was a safe position. (Back then, many people didn't own cribs. Babies slept on beds, often sharing them with their siblings.)

As she stepped out, she met a man who begged for a drink of water to revive himself. "I have to go across the way to the grocer," she said. "Wait here a moment and I'll be right back. Then you can come home with me for some water."

He pleaded with her. "I'm terribly thirsty. Can't you give me a drink now and then go to the store? I can't wait. I feel faint."

She couldn't ignore such a heartfelt appeal and returned home to bring him a glass of precious water.

As soon as she entered the apartment, she gave a scream. The baby was not where she had left her! She ran to the bed and saw that the baby had fallen into the water basin! My grandmother rushed over and pulled her out. A few minutes later would have been too late to save her life!

She then filled a glass with water and ran out to the man who was waiting longingly for a drink to revive himself. She searched high and low but couldn't find him. He had disappeared from sight.

It was then that she realized that Hashem had sent him as a good messenger to save her daughter's life. Having fulfilled his mission — he had vanished.

That baby was my mother…

The merit of that *mitzvah*, of helping a fellow Jew, had saved the life of the infant that would grow up and marry my father, Maran *Harav* Elyashiv, and bring me into this world.

When this story was told at the time to the Rav of Yerushalayim, *Hagaon* R' Tzvi Pesach Frank *zt"l*, he announced, "She will yet marry the future *gadol hador.*"

And indeed, his *berachah* came true completely.

The Jewelry Lost at the Beach

ONE OF THE WOMEN who comes to me frequently told me the following story which happened to her recently. It exemplifies the power of *tzedakah* and of unquestioning faith in our Torah leaders.

This woman went to a hotel near the Dead Sea together with her sister and several other women to benefit from its famous beneficial properties. When she arrived at the beach, she suddenly realized that she had forgotten to remove her jewelry and leave it in her hotel room. She didn't want to bathe in the salt water with it, nor did she wish to return all the way to the hotel. Her only solution was to remove the items and put them in the pocket of her bathrobe.

They spent the afternoon in the water and on the beach, and when it started to get dark, they all prepared to return to the hotel. Just then, the woman remembered that her jewelry was still in her robe, and she quickly put her hand in the pocket to make sure the items were still there. They weren't — the pocket was empty. The jewelry must have fallen out somewhere on the beach.

She was beside herself with anguish and guilt. The pieces were very expensive, not to mention their sentimental value. She did not give up hope altogether but began scouring the beach frantically, hoping to find the pieces in the sand. The other women joined her in the search but soon despaired of finding the jewelry.

One by one, the women gave up the search and returned to the hotel while the owner remained behind with another two or three women. After extensive efforts, she decided to make peace with the sad loss and return as well. As she was about to leave the shore, an unfamiliar woman approached her and said, "Did you ever hear of the special *segulah* for finding lost items? One pledges a sum for the soul of R' Mordechai Ber of Amsterdam and then prays that in the merit of that *tzedakah* the lost item will be found."

"You should know," she added, "that this wonderful *segulah* was publicized with much effort by the famous *tzaddik* R' David Leib Schwartz *zt"l* of Bnei Brak."

The mention of this name rang a bell in the distraught woman's mind.

Of all people, she remembered that *tzaddik*. She had lived in his vicinity as a child and had been fascinated by his figure, often staring intently at him whenever she saw him. R' David Leib had made it a steady practice to attend every public gathering — be it a *simchah* or a funeral — along with his *tzedakah pushke*. He would rattle it in front of people's faces and ask them to put a coin in the box for the poor, heaping many heartfelt blessings upon them in his unique, charming manner.

After he died, this woman used to visit his grave every year on his *yahrzeit*. And now, when she heard his name mentioned, she gave a start. Today was the day of his *yahrzeit* — the sixteenth of Kislev!

Having known in advance that she wouldn't be able to visit the grave this year, she had asked her husband to go there in her place.

Now her eyes lit up. Here was hope! She quickly made a pledge to give money for the soul of R' Mordechai Ber of Amsterdam, and a load lifted from her heart.

She was convinced that this pledge, coupled with the precise timing on the *yahrzeit* of the very man who had made this *segulah* public and spread it to so many people, would bring positive results and that she would find her jewelry.

After all, she had prayed by R' Dovid Leib's graveside year after year, and even sent her husband there in her stead to pray for the family and for *Klal Yisrael*. Who knows. she thought, whether the amazing reminder had not been Heaven-sent?

The probability of her finding the jewelry now, after a long and thorough search by so many women, and in the dark of night, seemed extremely slim, but the woman did not lose hope. She went back to the hotel to bring a powerful flashlight and returned with her sister to renew the search along the deserted shore.

Suddenly, the sister gave a cry, "I found it!"

Indeed, she had found the lost items of jewelry, all intact.

When the woman returned to Bnei Brak, she rushed over to tell me the story. I was deeply moved and shared her joy. I couldn't help but be impressed by the tremendous power of the *mitzvah* of *tzedakah*.

The Amazing Watch

I ALWAYS SAY THAT the *mitzvah* of *tzedakah* does not go un-
rewarded — one never loses by giving, as the following story
about helping a needy bride will beautifully illustrate:

In a distant community in South Africa lived a *tzaddik*,
Hagaon Rav Aharon Feufer *zt"l*, who was an outstanding
and very active leader of his *kehillah*.

A young girl once came to his house, dissolved in tears.
Between wracking sobs she managed to tell him that she
was an orphan *kallah* about to get married. She had just
received a gold piece of jewelry from her *chasan*, but as was
the custom, she was expected to give him a gold watch as
well. She had no money to buy such an expensive thing,
however, and was at a total loss.

Was there any way she could save her pride? Could the
Rav help her with her predicament?

Rav Feufer's heart went out to this orphan. He searched
among his personal belongings and found the gold watch he
had received as a *chasan*. He polished it well until it looked
like new, then wrapped it up handsomely and gave it to her
to give to her *chasan*. She wiped away her tears and went
joyfully off to give the gift.

Rav Feufer was very glad that he had been able to help

this orphan, but suddenly, a thought struck him. What would he tell his wife? The watch had been her gift to him. At some point, she would probably ask where the watch was and wonder to where it had disappeared. Not only had it cost her dearly, but she had given it with all her heart!

Rav Feufer decided that he had to replace it. He went to a friend, borrowed $2,000 and picked out a similar watch at a local jeweler. As he was standing on line by the cashier, he began asking himself how he would possibly be able to pay back that large sum. He turned the matter over in his mind but did not regret his noble deed for a moment.

Just as his turn came to pay for the watch, there was an announcement over the loudspeaker in the shop. The millionth customer of this very popular jewelry shop would be awarded his purchase for free, and the gentleman standing by the cash register was that lucky customer!

At first, Rav Feufer was too immersed in his thoughts to pay attention, but then he saw everyone staring at him and realized that he was that millionth customer! He would be getting a $2,000 gold watch for free!

An amazing story of how *tzedakah* for helping an orphan bride was repaid so very quickly!

My Sister Leah's Wonderful Children

MY SISTER, REBBETZIN LEAH Auerbach *a"h*, was not blessed with children of her own, but she did, in fact, raise entire generations of children orphaned from a mother or father. These children had been growing up in poor, disadvantaged conditions and their surviving parent had been unable to properly care for them. These unfortunates found a welcome refuge in the open home of *Hagaon* R' Ezriel Auerbach *shlita* and his Rebbetzin, Leah. They opened their hearts as well and showered love and care upon their foster children.

My sister had a very sick neighbor who was unable to take care of her own children because of her sad condition. Rebbetzin Leah gathered them into her home as well and tended to them with the same loving attention as the orphans. When they grew up and reached marriageable age, she was there for them, and married them off at her own expense, each in turn. Who can say that all these children were not like her own natural offspring, if not more?

My sister Leah passed away almost at the same time as my sister-in-law, Ahuva Berman *a"h*. I couldn't help comparing them and thinking about them. These two women are surely sitting close to one another in *Gan Eden*. It is interesting to note that both of them suffered from a stomach disease that is known to be "the sickness of *tzaddikim*," and both of them passed away on *erev* Shabbos — another indication of their righteousness. May their souls be bound up together with all the *tzaddikim* and *tzidkaniyos* in *Gan Eden*!

Every Thursday, Rebbetzin Kanievsky prepared a challah dough from which she separated challah in the most excellent way (hidur). Many women came to participate in the ceremony, giving her kvitlach notes with their names and requests for blessings in various areas. The photo shows the Rebbetzin's kitchen right before the hafrashas challah rite.

Separating Challah

Every Week Anew

AN ACQUAINTANCE WHO LIVES in Bnei Brak occasionally attended the *vasikin* prayers in the women's section of the Lederman shul.

This woman also pays me a visit at my home at a set day each year in order to recite "*Nishmas*" with great fervor, thereby thanking Hashem for the special miracle which she experienced at that time of the year, when her life was in danger.

The incident took place over fifteen years ago. The woman had just experienced a very difficult birth and there were complications. She lay in critical condition in the Intensive Care Unit, her life hanging by a thin thread.

Her parents rushed over to our house and described the dire situation.

My husband, R' Chaim, advised them to add the name "Chaya" to their daughter's name, and I told them that they should have their daughter commit herself to the *mitzvah* of *hafrashas challah* each week.

In the end, I went to the hospital myself and asked her directly if she was ready to undertake this obligation.

All she could do was nod, and she did so.

Later on, after she recovered, she related what had gone

through her mind at that very moment: What a small price to "pay," she had thought, in exchange for receiving the gift of life!

Thursday came around and the woman's mother arrived at her hospital room bearing a large bowl of dough. She separated a piece from it and gave it to her daughter to recite the blessing over it.

On the following day, miraculously enough, the doctors were able to pinpoint the exact problem. She received treatment accordingly and her recovery from then on was very speedy. Within several days she was able to leave the hospital, whole and healthy.

Many women heard about this miracle and resolved to begin practicing *hafrashas challah* as well, week in and week out, or at least before each Shabbos *Mevorchim* (the Shabbos before Rosh Chodesh).

True to her commitment to the valued *mitzvah* of taking *challah*, this woman has kept her promise, year after year — every *erev* Shabbos.

And each year, around the time that the miracle took place, she comes to my house with copies of a special prayer she had printed up, and hands them out to all the women present. When said at the time of *hafrashas challah*, this prayer is conducive to meriting sons who are *tzaddikim*.

Hafrashas Challah Brings Heavenly Aid

BEFORE ROSH HASHANAH ONE year, I broke my hand and couldn't function normally. That year, Shabbos followed right after Rosh Hashanah, so that it was like a three-day Yom Tov. And there I was, my hand in a cast, beset by pain and unable to move.

One of my main concerns was the thought that I would not be able to perform the *mitzvah* of *hafrashas challah*. How could I forfeit this *mitzvah* which I was so careful in keeping every week? I *davened* that Hashem find a solution for me.

Thursday arrived and with it, a knock on the door. I opened it to find a neighbor standing there. This is what she had to say: "With the big Yom Tov coming up, I already baked *challos*; but today I was suddenly afraid that it might not be enough, so I put up another batch of dough. Then I thought to myself, 'I've already performed the *mitzvah* and said the blessing. Why shouldn't I go and look for someone who hasn't made *hafrashas challah* and let her have the merit? Would you like to do it?'"

How happy I was! For several weeks afterwards, this dear friend and neighbor prepared an extra batch of dough so that I would have the *mitzvah*, despite my broken hand.

In the Merit of Hafrashas Challah

THERE WAS A PERIOD when I wasn't feeling well. One night I had a dream.

An elderly woman appeared to me and said, "Go to a certain bakery not far from your home every day, from Sunday through Thursday, and separate the required *challah* measure from their dough; if you take the trouble to do so, you will be healthy again."

I awoke and realized that it had been a dream — but I did not take it lightly.

I began going to that bakery, day after day, and separating the *challah* from the dough. Sure enough, my health improved, and I felt much, much better.

Added Life

WHEN I WAS A young wife, I lived near Rebbetzin Nadel, wife of *Hagaon* R' Gedalya *zt"l*. She was expecting then, and when the time came for her to give birth, she was very apprehensive and refused to go to the hospital.

Her husband felt that she should go, and he asked me to convince her that it was the right thing to do.

I went to her and she told me that during the course of the birth of her previous child, she had experienced clinical death. She told me that in her state of near death, a voice said to her, "Know that your time on earth was up and you were supposed to go up to Heaven, but you are being given a reprieve. Why? Because you feared that the wheat being sold during this *shemittah* year was not procured from a source that was careful to keep the laws of *shemittah* according to Hashem's will.

"Also, since you were careful all year long with your *challah* baking, and went out of your way to obtain flour that was completely free from all doubt concerning the prohibitions of *shemittah*, and was perfectly kosher by the highest standard — in that merit you are being granted additional years of life."

That is what the figure told her in the dream while she

was hovering between life and death. Now she turned to me and said, "I am about to give birth again, and this time I am very frightened because of that experience."

I tried to reassure her. "But you are still very careful in keeping the *mitzvah* of *hafrashas challah*, week in and week out. Surely Hashem will have mercy on you and in the merit of this *mitzvah*, He will sustain you, just as He did last time. I am convinced that you have nothing to worry about.

Baruch Hashem, she gave birth and everything went well, just as I had said.

It Protects from Sin

MANY STRANGE, FRIGHTENING THINGS happened to my family during the year of the Six Day War.

A bookcase toppled over in my mother-in-law's home.

My husband, the Rav, broke his foot and I had to be by his side almost all the time in order to help him and tend to his needs.

My dear and worthy neighbor, the wife of *Hagaon* R' Gedalya Nadel, passed away. Not long afterwards, her six-year-old son was involved in a serious traffic accident and hovered between life and death. I sat by his bedside in the hospital for a week.

All in all, that year was very difficult, with one tragedy following swiftly after another. I couldn't help reflecting about these trying situations and attempted to make some order in my mind.

I, myself, was just before the birth of my daughter, and I resolved that after I gave birth and all went well, I would bake *challos* each week with the required amount so that I could separate *challah* with a *berachah*.

My daughter was born without any complications, *baruch Hashem*. Now came the time for me to keep my promise.

When my friends heard about my resolution, they

suggested that I go to a bakery near my home and ask if I could separate *challah* once a week. Preparing a large dough each week was, after all, a major undertaking. But I was determined to take pains for this *mitzvah* and go to the trouble of baking my own *challos*.

Interestingly, we found out on the first Thursday evening that the bakery where I could have gone to simplify the *mitzvah* had discovered a hole in their sifter [and there was the possibility that bugs or worms could have made it into the dough].

Ever since then, to this very day, my husband refuses to eat bakery *challos* and only eats those which I have personally sifted the flour, separated *challah* and baked myself.

This goes to show how powerful is the *mitzvah* of *hafra-shas challah*. It is capable of protecting one from sinning...

This is the entrance to the women's section of the Lederman shul. The sign requests that women who wish to enter be dressed modestly.

הכניסה
 בית-הכנסת
אך ורק
לבוש צנוע

כניסה
לעזרת נשים
ולאולם שמחות
לנשים בלבד

מפני כבוד הרב שליט"א וחברנית תלמי"א,
מבקשים בכל לשון של בקשה
להגיע בלבוש צנוע
(חצאית ארוכה ובגדים סגורים ורחבים)
לפי רוח המקום.

Modesty and Sanctity

A Place of Kedushah
Makes a Difference

THE FOLLOWING STORY INVOLVES a woman who was completely secular — in outlook and dress. One day, she burst into the full waiting room and pushed her way to the threshold of my private room.

"My mother is very ill!" she shouted to the astonished women around her. "I don't have time to wait my turn. I have to go in immediately!"

Despite her shouting and pushiness, she did not get her way. Before her turn came around, it was time for *Maariv*, which takes precedence over everything else for me. I never miss *davening Maariv* with a *minyan*.

I suggested that she join the prayers but in order to do so, she would have to cover herself modestly before entering the women's section. I gave her one of my robes, and thus attired, she followed me down to the shul.

She sat down inside the women's section and looked around in fascination. She studied the women who were *davening* there, transfixed.

After the *davening*, I spoke with the women who were present and told over stories of *tzaddikim,* which we then discussed together. Finally, I was able to turn my attention to the secular visitor. She poured out her troubles while I listened attentively. Then I blessed her and expected her to get up and leave, but she wouldn't budge. Minutes ticked by and still she would not get up to go.

"Aren't you in a hurry to go someplace?" I asked pleasantly. "You said before that you didn't have time to wait your turn."

"I can't return home the same way I came," she said very emotionally. "After all I've seen and heard, I have to change. I have to become more modest in my appearance."

I rummaged around in my closet and found a new blouse. I gave it to her as a gift and she put it on very gratefully. Now she could return home, dressed properly.

See the tremendous power of *kedushah!* Just sitting in shul had made an impression upon her soul and ignited the spark which is latent in every Jew, no matter how distant they are from *Yiddishkeit*.

Leg Pain

THERE WAS A WOMAN who suffered excruciating pain in her legs and came to me for a blessing. She was not wearing stockings.

I said to her, "You must begin covering your feet with stockings. When you do, you will experience relief and see *yeshuos*." The woman resolved to do so and as soon as she put them on that day, the pain stopped.

Time passed and when she saw that she was better, she decided not to wear stockings anymore.

Sure enough, the pains returned and she came back to tell me that huge sores had suddenly developed on her bare legs. They were so raw and painful that they couldn't even be bandaged.

I explained that these were a result of her having stopped wearing stockings. She must resolve to put them on again and keep her legs properly covered at all times. As soon as she did, she would experience relief.

And so it was. As soon as she put on stockings, the sores healed, and she promised to continue wearing stockings.

When she came to me, we spoke in the presence of other women. There was a young woman in the room who wasn't wearing stockings at the time, either. When she heard the incredible story, she also resolved to put on stockings and wear them all the time. She was so firm in her resolution that she did not even want to go outside without them now in order to buy herself a pair in the neighborhood.

I brought her a clean pair of my own stockings which were very thick, but she didn't mind. She put them on and then went out to buy herself a supply of stockings, which she intended to wear from that time on.

Finding Lost Family in the Merit of Tzniyus

DURING WORLD WAR II, many Jewish children were hidden in Catholic monasteries throughout Europe and thus survived the war. Afterwards, the Jewish Agency tried to locate them to bring them back to their people and settle them in Eretz Yisrael.

Sadly enough, the agents were determined to place these children in the secular kibbutzim of Hashomer Hatzair, where every vestige of *Yiddishkeit* would be uprooted from their young souls.

Among the children brought to Eretz Yisrael was a little girl who came from a chareidi home where she had received a solid *chinuch*. Strong willed, she refused to eat the food which she knew was not kosher. Nor would she agree to wear the clothing that the kibbutz provided, because it was not modest.

The *madrichim* in the kibbutz tried to get her to wear pants. They did everything in their power to get her to compromise her level of *Yiddishkeit*, especially her *tzniyus* in dress, but she was adamant about wearing her only skirt at all times. She suffered ridicule and punishment, but nothing would make her swerve from her determination to maintain her principles.

An outing was planned one day for all the children of the kibbutz. Once again, the *madrich* tried to persuade her to give up her skirt and wear pants like all the other children, girls as well as boys. Our little heroine held her ground and refused.

Much against his will, the *madrich* decided to let her go on the outing nonetheless.

The children boarded the buses and not long afterwards the group arrived in Haifa. They were organized in one long line and marched through the streets. It was an unusual sight: hundreds of children dressed similarly and one lone girl wearing a skirt.

A chareidi woman happened to be on the street at the time and couldn't believe her eyes. What was that one religious girl doing amongst all those secular kibbutz children? She drew closer to satisfy her curiosity and suddenly, she gave a loud cry.

"Raizel! Aren't you Raizel, my sister's child?"

She ran to the girl, her lost niece, and gathered her into her arms, kissing her and hugging her tightly.

Raizel wept with surprise and joy at having found a dear relative — one who she had never even known existed. She had been so young, she did not remember her aunt.

"I knew that you had survived," the aunt exclaimed. "You are the only survivor from my sister's family. We searched all over for you, but couldn't find you."

It was only thanks to her strong will in maintaining her *tzniyus* that Raizel was finally reunited with her family and could return to observing the *mitzvos* according to her up-bringing. She was released from the kibbutz and went to live with her aunt. She grew up to be a noted Rebbetzin and a big *tzadekes.*

The Disease That Disappeared

ANOTHER SECULAR YOUNG WOMAN came to me, dressed very immodestly. She told me that she was suffering from a serious disease and that she was scheduled for a complicated surgery. Moreover, the doctors were not very optimistic that it would be successful.

She came to me as a last resort, hoping my blessing would help.

I asked her to tell me a little about herself. She told me about her weakness for new clothes; it was almost an addiction with her. Whenever she saw something nice in a shop window, she just had to go in and buy it.

I told her that Hashem wants women to dress modestly. I also told her that it was possible that her illness had come to shake her up and make her change her ways, especially in the area of dress.

A day before the surgery, she was admitted to the hospital and given a room. As she lay in the hospital bed, thoughts swirled around her head. Here she was, very ill, with a small chance of recovery, but she wanted very much to live.

All of a sudden, she leaped out of bed, got dressed and ran out of the hospital, without telling anyone, and went home. There, she sat and cried her heart out.

She prayed to Hashem, saying, "Hashem, I want to give You something, to make a sacrifice to You. I want to feel that I am giving You my whole life!"

She sat there for a long time but couldn't think of anything meaningful or exalted enough to offer as a sacrifice to Hashem.

Suddenly, her eyes lit up as a thought struck her. Now she knew! Her clothing — all of her immodest clothing. They would serve as her personal sacrifice.

She opened up her closet and looked at the improper clothing that filled it. She grabbed the whole lot in a big armful, went down to the yard, and set fire to them all.

This was truly a great sacrifice for her. It hadn't come easy, and now her closet was almost empty.

Having made her "sacrifice" to Hashem, her heart felt at ease. She went back to her hospital bed without telling anyone what she had just done.

The pre-surgical testing was resumed the following morning. The doctor studied the results but couldn't believe his eyes. There must have been some mistake because all the tests showed no sign whatsoever of the disease. After a period of observation, she was declared well and released from the hospital to carry on with her life. All because of a tremendous sacrifice — all in the merit of *tzniyus!*

An Explosion Averted in the Merit of Tzniyus

THIS STORY TOOK PLACE a few days before Pesach. The newspapers that day had shocking headlines, telling of a miracle. A car bomb filled with a large amount of explosives had been discovered in Haifa and dismantled just in time to avoid a major tragedy. It had been planted near a very busy shopping mall.

It almost seemed that it was discovered by accident. Had it been set off as planned, a major catastrophe would have resulted, with hundreds injured or killed.

How had it been discovered in time? Who had tipped off the police?

A group of students from Tzefas had come to visit me. These were seminary girls originally from irreligious homes —girls finding their way back to Torah *Yiddishkeit*. One of the main purposes of their visit was to be strengthened in the area of modesty in dress.

I spoke to them about the importance of *tzniyus*. I told them how Hashem greatly favors modesty, adding that this *mitzvah* had the power to protect people from terrible diseases, misfortunes and even terrorist acts.

I told them about the terminally ill young woman and

how she had run away from the hospital and gone home. I vividly described how she decided to make a tangible sacrifice to Hashem and had taken all of her immodest clothing and burned them. Miraculously, her illness had suddenly disappeared, and she was declared completely well.

This true story had a tremendous impact upon my listeners and they, too, resolved to strengthen themselves by dressing even more modestly than before.

When they returned to Tzefas, they organized an assembly for all the students. Each girl was asked to return home and bring back as many items as she could which did not meet the standards of *tzniyus*.

All the clothing they brought was examined, and anything problematic was thrown right into the garbage. Many of the items disqualified were new clothes that had been bought for Yom Tov; nevertheless, they were thrown into the heap.

This was only part of the program. After casting away the improper clothing, the girls sat down and prayed to Hashem to help strengthen them in this important area.

The very next day, the shocking news rocked the city and the entire country: a devastating tragedy had been averted just in the nick of time. A car bomb filled with massive explosives had been discovered and dismantled very shortly before it was scheduled to go off in a very busy shopping center.

The girls felt that they knew in whose merit it had been found just in time. Each one felt as if she, personally, had saved many lives.

The next day, the girls came to me again. They came in a

van which contained huge garbage bags filled all the clothing they were throwing away. I was moved to tears, together with them.

"You see, girls, Hashem loves *tzniyus*!" I told them.

Here, in this small, simple but warm room is where Rebbetzin Kanievsky sat, receiving tens of thousands of women who came from all over the world to pour out their hearts before her.

Being Satisfied with the Minimum

The Taste of a Candy

WHEN MY SISTER-IN-LAW, REBBETZIN Ahuva Berman, was in the final stages of her terminal disease, she suffered, among other things, a bitter taste in her mouth and sought relief. The doctor suggested that she suck on a candy.

The Rebbetzin had not tasted a candy for the past thirty years. In general, she lived a very austere life, refraining from comforts and luxuries of all kinds. She ate the minimum needed to keep healthy and enable her to serve Hashem. Candies, certainly, were not part of her diet.

It was no simple matter for her to take a candy after having refrained from eating sweets for thirty years. She needed a special *hataras nedarim*, being absolved of a vow, to be able to eat a simple sucking candy!

The Same Dress

MY MOTHER HAD ONE dress for very special occasions — her children's wedding. She wore the same dress to each one, washing it right after the event and hanging it up in her closet afterwards until the next *simchah*.

The dress did not finish its duty when she had married off all her children. By then, there were the weddings of grandchildren, and she wore it to these as well.

One time, before a wedding of a granddaughter, the *kallah* asked her grandmother if she would agree to wear a new dress.

What was her reply? "And how do you think one can deserve a *chasan* who is a *ben Torah* if the wife is always buying new clothing?"

These are the sefarim from which Rebbetzin Kanievsky studied
and davened. Each night, her granddaughter would lay them out
so that when her grandmother awoke before dawn, she would be
able to fill her self-imposed daily quota before she began a very
full day speaking with her many visitors.

אגרת הרמב"ן

נשמת כל חי

ארחות צדיקים השלם

נצור לשונך מנוקד

מדריך להלכות לשון הרע

מתוק לפי לימוד יומי

מיוסד על ה"חפץ חיים"

הרבנית קנייבסקי

Yiras Shamayim

Extreme Vigilance Regarding Chametz

THIS STORY TOOK PLACE many years ago before Pesach. My sister-in-law, Rebbetzin Ahuva Berman, my husband's sister, bought herself new stockings for the upcoming Yom Tov.

Her purchase was put into a used plastic bag since, in those times, people — even stores — were very sparing with these. Storeowners would not think twice about reusing a bag. Rebbetzin Ahuva paid, returned home, and put the parcel away in her closet. She didn't need it until after the holiday began. On Chol HaMo'ed, she went to her closet to get the stockings. When she opened the bag, she gave a shriek.

The family rushed to her bedroom in alarm. Had something happened to her? They heard cries from the closet. Perhaps there was a snake in there (which was possible since they lived on the ground floor)?

They tried to make sense of the garbled words stammered between hysterical weeping. After a long while, she calmed down enough to explain why she was so upset.

When she had opened the bag to take out the new stockings, what should she find in it but half a pretzel!

Chametz on Pesach!

For three years after that very traumatic event, the Rebbetzin would not allow a pretzel to cross her threshold; she was still so shaken up.

The shock lingered on even after that, for when she finally agreed to let her children eat those salty treats, they were not allowed to eat the kind with the twisted or round shape, only pretzel sticks.

Remove Your Shoes

A CERTAIN JEW ONCE left Eretz Yisrael to travel abroad and raise some money to help marry off his daughter. He went from place to place, house to house, but all he received were small coins. Helpful people advised him to go to a neighboring country to try his luck there. And so he did.

When he arrived at his destination, the airport authorities at passport control told him to remove his shoes for inspection — all foreign nationals were asked to do so. When he tried to put on his shoes again, he discovered that his were gone. Apparently, another passenger had taken his shoes and left his own by mistake.

The other pair of shoes had probably belonged to a gentile, as they had crosses etched on them — something that he refused to wear. He wouldn't have taken those shoes in any case because they didn't belong to him.

He left the airport in his stocking-feet. Just then, a fellow Jew approached him. "Is your situation so desperate that you can't afford to buy a pair of shoes?" he asked somewhat skeptically but also in concern.

After the visitor explained what had happened, the man remarked, "Are you so determined not to wear shoes that have the symbol of a cross that you go out in your socks?"

Without waiting for an answer, he asked again, "What brings you to this country, anyway?"

"I've come here to try my luck in collecting charity to help me marry off my daughter."

The stranger was so deeply moved and impressed by the Yerushalmi Jew that he gave him a large sum of money on the spot.

The message is two-fold: A person should always adhere to his principles, and he will not lose out by being truthful. The result may not be obvious right away, but eventually it will become clear.

Opposite the fruit trees in the garden of the house on Rechov Rashbam. Here is where Rebbetzin Kanievsky recited birkas ha'ilanos each year at the beginning of Nisan.

Blessings

Afikoman from the Chazon Ish

I SPENT MY FIRST Seder night as a young wife together with my husband's uncle, the Chazon Ish.

My sister-in-law, Rebbetzin Ahuva Berman, still a young girl, decided she would steal the *afikoman*. When the time came to eat it at *nirtzah*, the Chazon Ish demanded gently, "Bring the *afikoman* now so that we can eat it."

She refused to give it up without making a bargain.

"I want you to bless me that I'll have children who will be *tzaddikim*."

Maran the Chazon Ish blessed her as she had requested.

To be sure, her children were all *tzaddikim* and *talmidei chachamim*.

Here was a wise girl who knew what to ask for from the Chazon Ish.

A New Hospital

THE BNEI BRAK HOSPITAL Maayanei Hayeshuah is celebrating its twentieth year. I can remember its early beginnings.

Two of my daughters were about to give birth. There was no question that they would go to the new chareidi hospital in Bnei Brak — Maayanei Hayeshuah.

One of them was willing and eager to register there, but the other one had serious reservations. "It's still a very new hospital and I am not familiar with how it operates. I don't know the nurses or the doctors, and I'm really nervous about the whole thing…" she murmured.

My husband said to her, "When the time comes for you to have your baby, there will have been so many births already that the corridors will be filled for lack of room!"

True to his prediction, my daughter was taken to the hospital on Rosh Hashanah, and that happened to be a very busy time. For lack of accommodation, the halls were indeed lined with occupied hospital beds — the overflow from the already packed rooms.

Sheva Berachos

THERE WAS ONCE A Jew with seven daughters, all of them already of marriageable age, but none of them yet engaged.

He also had a son, a scholarly *yeshiva bachur* of nineteen with an excellent reputation. He came to his father one day with astonishing news: "The Rosh Yeshiva called me over today and said he has a fine *shidduch* for me."

The father was not pleased at all, and contrary to what his son had thought, he replied angrily, "Aren't you ashamed of yourself? Here you are with seven sisters ahead of you and you want to skip over them all and get married first?"

The young man saw things differently. Some of his sisters were already a bit older, with dwindling hopes of finding a match. Was he expected to wait for all of them to get married before he himself got married? After some discussion, they decided to ask my husband what to do.

My husband uttered the following simple statement [which turned out to be a blessing as well]: "*Berachah v'hatz-lachah!*" The father did not argue but went ahead with the match suggested by the Rosh Yeshiva, and it wasn't long before the son got married.

I met the family fourteen months later returning from the *sheva berachos* of their seventh daughter!

Seven blessings indeed!

A Son and Two Daughters

A WOMAN WHOSE INFANT had just died, came to me in tears, hoping to receive some comfort.

I blessed her heartily that in the following year she would give birth to twins.

Her husband was with her at the time. When he heard the blessing, he went to the Rav to confirm and reinforce my words.

My husband smiled and said, "The Rebbetzin said twins? I bless you that by next year you will have triplets!"

His blessing, which I believe included mine as well, came true. The following year the woman gave birth to a son and two daughters.

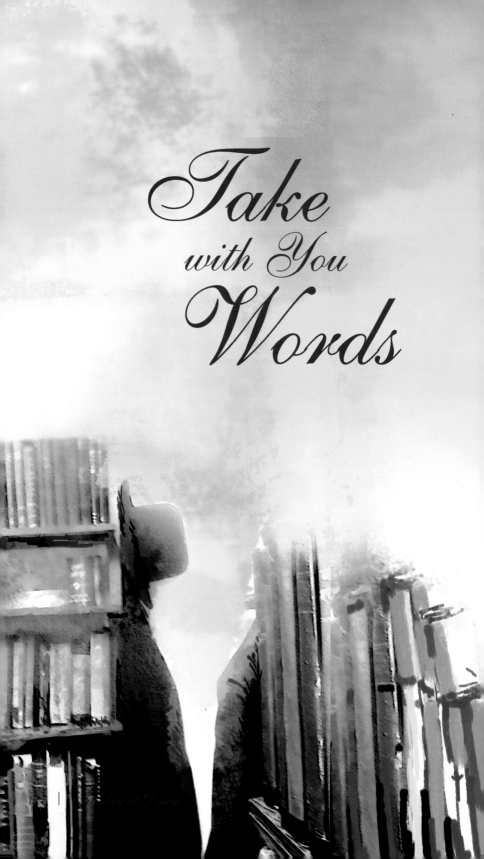

*T*he silence of a pre-dawn
On a Tuesday morn
Prayers already rising
From the Rebbetzin — not surprising.

In the women's section
Slipping in quietly without detection
Another, watching with awe
Listening, absorbing everything she saw.

An amazing figure, the Rebbetzin, yet that's no surprise
From generations of *tzaddikim* she did rise
In a home of Torah she was reared
So, too, in her home Hashem was revered.

After prayers she is flanked
By indebted devotees who thank
For every iota of inspiration
To meet the new day with holy rededication.

They are reinforced with love for Torah each day
With *emunah* every step of the way
To help, encourage and if need be yield
Lips used for holiness — from evil talk sealed.

Take her words and her holy speech
Internalize her lessons, to Hashem beseech
That from each message, each story to learn
And thus, eternal life to earn.

Valuable Advice from the Rebbetzin

DAY AFTER DAY, WOMEN came to the Rebbetzin for advice and to receive her blessings. They unburdened themselves to her, telling her of their troubles or of their physical aches and pains.

Like a loving, caring mother, the Rebbetzin listened with her ears and her heart, hoping to be able to soothe their suffering in some way. Some of her advice came directly from the *gemara* or from *Chazal*'s teachings. There were *segulos* she had heard from her father-in-law, the Steipler, or from her husband *ylcht"a*. She believed in them implicitly as being tried and effective — for health and cures — and she dispensed them with love and conviction that they would help those who followed them.

It was truly heartwarming to see the Rebbetzin's utter joy whenever someone came back to her to report the success of her good advice — how the pain had disappeared and the woman had been cured, with the help of Hashem.

I have compiled some of the *eitzes* and *segulos* which she dispensed very often — some of which I heard directly from her, while others were told to me by the Rebbetzin's close family members.

Yeshuah for Everything That Ails

The Rebbetzin was very careful to study each and every day two *halachos* on *shemiras halashon*, guarding one's tongue. In her sweet, charming manner, she frequently advised the women who came to her to do the same. "I read this particular *segulah* in the work of Rav Segal of Manchester, and it is a very worthwhile practice to follow..."

Conquering Anger

The Rebbetzin always advised people to work on eliminating anger. Her suggestion was to study and recite the *Iggeres HaRamban* which deals with this issue; she promised that it would help to overcome that negative trait.

For *Refuos*

When people came to the Rebbetzin telling her about a sick person who needed a *refuah*, she would tell the family of the patient to study *Maseches Kinim* as a tried *segulah*.

Very often, the Rebbetzin herself would hand out copies of this *masechta* to the family.

Against *Ayin Hara*

Some people are afraid of the evil eye put on them by others. When such people came to her with this fear, she had a ready remedy: to read the *parshah* found in the *siddur* after *Shacharis*: "*Nega tzara'as...*," which is taken from *Vayikra*. She confided that she said it herself to avoid an *ayin hara*.

For Success

The Rebbetzin did not only deal with blessings for sick people. Many came to her for a blessing asking for success, before taking a decisive step in their lives. She related to every request with her full attention and characteristic warmth. She would always add that the best advice for Heavenly help was to firmly declare: "*Hashem Hu HaElokim — Ein od Milvado.*" This is a tried and proven *segulah* from R' Chaim Volozhin and is known to effect wonders.

After Birth or a *Yeshuah*

The Rebbetzin was a firm believer in the importance of reciting "*Nishmas*" after one experienced something good in their lives. She herself said it every day and would distribute printed pamphlets of this prayer to many of the women who came to her. She especially encouraged them to say it after birth or at any special good event they experienced in their lives.

For a General Boost

Not everyone had a specific request to make. Some women simply wanted a general boost, a *chizuk* — a suggestion on how to improve themselves.

The Rebbetzin used to tell them, "Add another prayer each day, beyond what you are used to saying, and say it from the *siddur*. You will see *yeshuos*."

A Gutte Voch

Do you want to have a good week? The Rebbetzin had a good suggestion for this, too. She urged people to wash for *melaveh malkah* and to drink something hot. They were to repeat the words of the *gemara*, "*Chamin b'motza'ei Shabbos melugma* — Something hot on *motza'ei Shabbos* is a remedy."

"My husband, the Rav, always washes his hands over bread for *melaveh malkah* immediately after *havdalah*," she would say.

After a Bad Dream

When people came to speak with her about a frightening dream they'd had, she would tell them of an important practice. In the *Birkas Kohanim* of *Musaf* on Shabbos or festivals, there is a special prayer found in the *siddur* to add which goes like this, "*Ribono shel Olam...* I belong to You and my dreams belong to You. I had a dream..." This short prayer can change the dream for the good.

A *Segulah* to Have Righteous Children

The Rebbetzin made a dough each Thursday of sufficient measure that she could separate *challah* from it with a *berachah*. She spoke a lot about this particular *mitzvah*, telling women that her husband, the Rav, said that the time when the *challah* is separated is a favorable one in Heaven; it is a time when one can bring about many *yeshuos*. It is also a special *segulah* for meriting children who are pure and righteous.

Medical Advice

How to Arrest Hair Loss (from the Steipler):

Ingredients: A tablespoon of olive oil, a tablespoon of castor oil, one egg yolk, a few drops of lemon.

Preparation: Blend all ingredients well.

Wash hair first with regular shampoo and rinse off. Shampoo with the oil mixture and leave on the head for twenty minutes, then rinse off. Repeat this procedure once a week for as long as is necessary, until marked improvement is shown.

Bedwetting

Ingredients: 1 pound radish, 1 pound parsley, ½ pound horseradish, 12 cups water.

Preparation: Boil all the ingredients together on a low flame for twelve hours. Pour the resulting liquid into nine glasses.

Drink three glasses a day for three days.

Remedy for Kidney Stones

Put into a blender: Watermelon with rind — enough to produce a liter and a half of liquid. Drink the liquid over the course of one day.

This juice cleanses the kidneys thoroughly and soothes any inflammation in that area.

In addition, it is advisable to drink a tablespoon of olive oil on an empty stomach each morning.

An Aid for an Easy Birth

Very close to the time of birth, the woman should take an *esrog* upon which the blessing was said on Sukkos, say the *berachah* "*Borei pri ha'eitz*" with deep *kavanah*, and eat from it.

(The Rebbetzin told me that after Sukkos she takes the *esrog* that the Rav used on Sukkos as well as *esrogim* from other *tzaddikim*, and makes preserves, which she puts into many small jars. She distributes them to women about to give birth, and they report back to her that these helped them very much.)

An Iron-Building Drink against Anemia

Ingredients: Three carrots, 1 small beet, 1 pepper, 1 cucumber, 1 apple.

Preparation: Liquify all the ingredients in a blender.

Drink the concoction every day. (The Rebbetzin said that it is advisable to prepare a fresh batch every day for the best effect. It is known to do wonders.)

Cough Medicine

Ingredients: Onion, a few spoons of honey.

Preparation: Dice the onion, add the honey and wait until the mixture dissolves. Take a spoonful every once in a while.

Relief from Asthma

Ingredients: One onion, two tablespoons sugar.

Preparation: Dice the onion in the morning and cover with the sugar. During the day, the onion will release its juice. Drink the liquid before sleeping and repeat every day until marked improvement is shown.

Relief for Sinusitis

Ingredients: One tablespoon of mustard seed (available in health food shops), one tablespoon flour, one tablespoon of boiling water.

Preparation: Mix the ingredients together. Smear the mitxture on a cloth and place on the forehead overnight.

Relief from Gum Inflammation

Take an onion, grate it or put it in a juicer to extract the liquid and gargle with juice it as often as you can. This is very effective.

Relief for the Flu

Ingredients: One teaspoon cinnamon, one teaspoon honey, juice of half a lemon, boiling water.

Preparation: Fill a glass with boiling water, add the above ingredients and mix, like tea. Drink as many glasses of this mixture as you can while suffering from the flu. As a preventive, one glass each morning is sufficient.

Relief for Earache

Peel a whole garlic clove and place it at the opening of the ear. The clove should be large enough that it won't accidentally enter the ear canal. The garlic will cause the pus to drain out and the pain to subside.

Here is the chair of Maran the Steipler, author of *Kehillos Yaakov*, and father-in-law of the Rebbetzin. When women came to her especially embittered and sorrowful, she would say to them, "Sit here and pray with all your heart. Recite *Nishmas* with deep *kavanah* and tell Hashem all of your troubles. From this place, your prayers will rise speedily and directly to Heaven, and your deliverance will be sure to come soon."

The Rebbetzin's only desire and yearning was to fortify dejected women and to channel blessing and goodness to them from Heaven. With her pure heart, she hoped to bring relief, bounty and *siyata diShmaya* to all who suffer in *Klal Yisrael*. Her sweet smile and pleasant words were directed at each person who came to her. She gave her whole self to others, as a gift, with devotion and sacrifice — everything for the Jewish daughters who so thirsted for her blessing and hung upon her every word.

We pray to merit carrying on and following her ways by absorbing and reflecting some of the great light which she radiated, by whispering with our lips those prayers which she urged women to say, by smiling to others and reflecting her great love. May we continue along the path which she tread and illuminated for us. May all this be for the merit of her pure and precious soul, *l'iluy nishmasah*.